Sydney

Other titles in this series

Forthcoming

Sydney

DELIA FALCONER

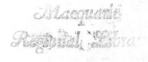

NEW
SOUTH

A New South book

Published by
University of New South Wales Press Ltd
University of New South Wales
Sydney NSW 2052
AUSTRALIA
www.unswpress.com.au

National Library of Australia
Cataloguing-in-Publication entry
    Author: Falconer, Delia
    Title: Sydney/Delia Falconer.
    ISBN: 978 192141 092 5 (hbk.)
    Series: Cities series; 3
    Subjects: Haunted places – New South Wales – Sydney.
        Sydney (N.S.W.) – History.
    Dewey Number: 994.41

Design Josephine Pajor-Markus
Cover design Sandy Cull, gogoGingko
Cover photography Ricky Price, rickyprice.com
Author photo Bronwyn Rennex
Endpaper map David Atkinson, handmademaps.com
Printer Everbest

This book is printed on paper using fibre supplied from plantation
or sustainably managed forests.

Contents

I looked out of my window in the dark
At waves with diamond quills and combs
  of light
That arched their mackerel-backs and
  smacked the sand
In the moon's drench, that straight enormous
  glaze,
And ships far off asleep, and Harbour-buoys
Tossing their fireballs wearily each to each,
And tried to hear your voice, but all I heard
Was a boat's whistle, and the scraping squeal
Of seabirds' voices far away, and bells,
Five bells. Five bells coldly ringing out.

Five bells.

— *from 'Five Bells' by Kenneth Slessor*

Foreword

In his memoir of living in Verona, English novelist Tim Parks suggests the Italian love of *la dolce vita* is not quite what it seems. As he was watching television footage of one of Italy's naval ships heading for Beirut on a UN mission, he recalls, the camera panned onto a young sailor calling back to shore. Was he shouting farewells to a girlfriend, or boyfriend, or uttering some howl of defiance? No, as the camera drew closer to his red face it became clear that he was tearfully mouthing the word 'Mamma'. Thus Parks makes his case. The Italians' casual cheer is only a front. They are essentially homebodies, disturbed by cuisine from another region, let alone any more drastic changes.

A similar case can be made for Sydney. From the outside it seems like the brashest and most superficial of cities, almost a kind of unplanned holiday resort. But perhaps you need to have grown up here, as I did, to see that its fundamental temperament is melancholy. Everything else is a side effect, a symptom of darker emotional currents that run so deep they are almost tectonic. Sydney may look golden, but this is the sunniness of Mozart, whose bright notes, especially at their most joyful, seem to cast themselves out across a great abyss.

Just the other day I was walking up the hill from my apartment at dusk when I saw a small silver car with a parking ticket on its windscreen. The envelope looked strange. When I got closer I saw that someone had written on it in black texta: *I just backed into your car, and now I'm pretending to write a note. FUCK YOU!* It wasn't hard to imagine the triple assault as the owner returned: horror at seeing the parking ticket, and the big dent from a four-wheel-drive's tow-bar in the bonnet, then relief on finding the note that turned quickly into outrage. 'My God, if you could do that you could rape someone', a Melbourne friend said, horrified. But there was a part of me that felt some base response of familiarity, even of pride. This was my town. It was a place you took lightly at your peril, whose beauty has never been far from rage, and perhaps even the urge for destruction.

Like Los Angeles, with which it is sometimes unfavourably compared, Sydney's misty sunshine is never far from noir. And like Los Angeles, an Art Deco golden age cast its features — its Bridge, its Luna Park, its mission-style mansions like 'Boomerang', its palms — into a smile. It has been as ravaged by the car, as dazzled by its improbable location, as prone to boosterism and corruption as Los Angeles. Its air can look as luminous and insubstantial. But to Deco lightness, in Sydney's case, you have to add sandstone as a kind of base note, an ever-present reminder of its Georgian beginnings and more ancient past. To that mix, again, you have to add water, which penetrates the city with bright fingers, filters constantly through its foundations, and weighs down the air. While Los Angeles' moments of darkness seem to come from a sense of dry ignition, an inkling that the city's desert winds, like the Santa Ana immortalised by Joan Didion, spark desperate acts, Sydney's seem more like the precipitation of something already moody and brooding, out of air that sweats. Similarly, Sydney's skies are so dense and changeable that it is hard to share Los Angeles' shock that evil activities could hide themselves under its calm, relentless sun. Any madness here feels more chthonic, something deeply buried that wells up. While for Didion, the key image of that Pacific city is the paper in her typewriter curling in the heat, my childhood memories are of the dark layer of black pollution and mould soaked into the sandstone fronts of Sydney's grand buildings, and the green trails of water leaking from the cliffs and high walls of the Rocks. That, and the great posts of the ferry jetties that always seemed to be decomposing before one's eyes in the jellyfish-filled water, with their smell of brine and rot.

Yet for all the accusations of brainlessness made against them, both cities are where you will find the most feral, interesting thinkers. This was one of my first impulses, in taking on this project — to try to come to grips with how people have thought and dreamed here, to confound the prejudice that this is a shallow place that generates more heat than light. With its love of eccentrics and poets, Sydney has a more paradoxical, more visionary, even more iconoclastic, intellectual history than that of any other Australian city. Yet at the same time, and this is part of its paradoxical nature, you would be hard-pressed to find elsewhere thinkers as palpably earth-bound. My thoughts turned to the writers Kenneth Slessor, Patrick White and Ruth Park, who took the city's grimy pulse from its stained footpaths and shabby terraces. I recalled First Fleet Lieutenant William Dawes, whose notebooks recording the Eora language began with strict grammars only to flare out into jottings about blowing out candles and touching hands.

Think in Sydney and you can be no cold metaphysician. The material constantly intrudes – even as I write, a pulpy smell of iodine from the over-warm February harbour comes through the window – and this freights every one of its books, paintings and conversations. Even a walk up the street is often literally 'up', as the city climbs to precipitous cliffs at its sea edge, in contrast to a metropolis like Manhattan where every rise and declivity has been razed. Yet this constant awareness of the material, which goes back to our Georgian past and its interest in the body's humours like bile and phlegm, is quite different from shallow materialism. In fact, paying close attention to the city's tides and sunlight can even constitute an antidote to the city's pretensions to glamour; at the very least it gives our appetites an edge. The distinction is hard for outsiders to grasp.

It almost feels unusual, in this rapidly growing city, to have been born here; even more unusual to have ancestors on my father's side, if family legend is to be believed, who go all the way back to the First Fleet. Lieutenant William Dawes, whose tiny observatory gave Dawes Point its name, is supposed to be a distant ancestor – though much as I long for this to be true, my fear that it probably is not has made me shy away from genealogical research. I am unusually lucky, though I did not entirely feel this at the time, to have had what was in many ways an Edwardian childhood in McMahons Point, with parents who were at once bohemian and puritan, modern in child-rearing philosophy but untouched by fad and fashion. I kept company with much older people for the first seven years of my life. My paternal grandmother, with whom I was most close, was born in 1886 in Windsor, then a country town, only

moving to Drummoyne when she and my grandfather married; with the unthinking pragmatism
of an era, the inmates of the Gladesville Asylum
down the road had been employed to make her
bouquet of white lilies. This gentle woman would
be buried from the same tiny Gladesville church in
1984 at the age of ninety-eight, and I remember,
as the funeral cortege wound its way to the Field
of Mars cemetery in Ryde, an old man standing at
attention on the footpath with his hat held to his
chest. He would be long dead now, along with this
touching custom.

Both my English grandfathers had jumped
ship in Sydney, both from the Merchant Navy. I
never knew them, though I grew up with a handful
of stories about young boy apprentices crying as
they climbed the rigging of windjammers struggling around Cape Horn. Both apparently excelled
at sewing, a forgotten sailor's craft. My maternal
grandmother was born in Chile. She and my
grandfather must have stood out on the streets of
circumspect 1930s Sydney, he a mine manager in
white Palm Beach suits, she tiny and imperious
with her tailored jackets and penetrating accent:
I will always think of perfumed frangipanis in
bloom as her *frangi-pangies*. After his death she

would join the ranks of lonely widows who then populated the inner eastern suburbs like Darling Point, dying of gas inhalation when she suffered a heart attack and the milk she was warming boiled over on the stove — the kitchen window carefully locked against the thieves who had been targeting the flat. Almost every day I walk under her brown block of units, in the street that bears the area's original Eora name, and on, past the art nouveau walls and turreted gatehouses of long-gone estates, now replaced by the apartment blocks that bear their names: 'Hopewood', 'Longwood' and 'Babworth'.

But I am aware that my family's long relationship with the city may make me the least qualified person to write about it. Its new energy can probably be most strongly felt at its bursting edges, at those new estates clustering round the early colonial outposts of Windsor and Campbelltown, whose fresh grids can be seen cutting into the bush and farmland as your plane descends into Mascot airport. Instead, I can't help looking backwards, especially to my own childhood, during that quiet but ambivalent time before the new wave of international investment came to town. With that money would come wider horizons, new food, friends from other places. But it also set off the city's craven addiction to glitter, which would lead playwright David Williamson to curse it with the title 'Emerald City'. I would not want to return to that dull Sydney I inhabited when I was sixteen and walked through lifeless Martin Place on my way home from Saturday acting classes at the Phillip Street Theatre; though perhaps I would stop the clock a few years later in the early eighties, when the new Writers' Festival was held in the dim bowels of the Town Hall and the Balmain writers were drunk onstage, and in fact the whole city was slightly drunk on naïvely imagining what it might become.

It is no coincidence that I had just started university then and was also imagining the shape my own life would take. Ask anyone who lives in a large city to describe 'their' town and it will probably be the city of their early twenties, when their generation seemed to own it; but in my generation's case, for a little while, when the inner city was a ruin, we really did. At the same time I know that my own Sydney, like everyone's, is partly imaginary; and I have come to see more and more that I came to know it at the tail end of its most culturally Protestant moment, when it had closed itself off from the wider world after the excesses of the Second World War and was trying its hardest to be English. It began to wake up just as I left school; but until then, although in many ways crimped and constraining, it was also a lovely empty place whose sunstruck streets and parks seemed mesmerised by light. Part of the pleasure and challenge of writing this book has been grappling with my own 'Protestant dreaming'. I still feel the city's old gravitational pull toward plainness and restraint, which might pass by those who have not lived here long, or, if they do feel its hard edge, they may dismiss it as random. Yet this secret rigidity is one reason for Sydney's perverse love of the mad and feral, even if it often sets out to crush eccentrics and make them conform. We are a contradictory city.

More than that – we are the most dialectical of cities, a place of wrestling and opposite forces. Sydney's restless to-and-fro energy comes out of a nagging sense that something is missing, even, or perhaps particularly, when the city is at its most soft-aired and shiny. This feeling has many causes, which it has been my impulse to try to uncover. The first of these is the destruction of the language and culture of the Eora before the loss could even be grasped. This was a human tragedy. It was also the cause of an existential dilemma. For to live here is always to feel the place has a secret life that resists you. This sense of hauntedness is not necessarily always conscious, but expresses itself in our tendency to judge, to boast, to act out, to bully, to look for visions; or, failing that, to revel in the city's sweat and grit. Almost all of Sydney's emotions, even the most violent, can be traced back to a longing, which sometimes seems to have an almost geographic force. When we love it, that love is aching. Even our famed showiness is driven by a sense of loss. This overcompensation makes Sydney the most dynamic of cities, although it can agitate at such a high vibration as to appear almost still, to masquerade as torpid.

True to this spirit, I love and hate the place at once. But on nights like the summer evening earlier this year when I walked home through a limpid dusk, all is forgiven – its brutishness, its piggish bus drivers, its violent moods. As I set out from the city's southern end, the sandstone walls beneath the Central railway line still held the day's heat. The neon sign above Wentworth Avenue had gone from Sharpie's golf house, but I remembered the little golfer who used to guide his golden chip-shot, endlessly, towards the nineteenth hole.

In Darlinghurst I passed a row of old terraces where feral banana trees had colonised the tiny courtyards behind them, and walked on, past the smell of Thai food, up dirty William Street. Outside my flat the flying foxes were landing in the Moreton Bay fig, and already their squabbles had sent a thick fall of fruit onto the pavement, which smelled phlegmy and sweet in the dew. The moon rose from the invisible harbour into a sky of such a deep royal blue it was almost hard to believe in. The street smelled of low tide. For all its beauty, the city could return in an instant to pulp. And that thought was strangely cheering.

Ghosting

This is my favourite Sydney story. For a few decades, in the middle of last century, a hospital on the north shore sent each mother of a newborn home with a jacaranda seedling. And so when the valleys on either side of the city's train lines flare violet in October and November, each bright burst represents the beginning of a life. I was born in the old Crown Street Hospital in Surry Hills, long since demolished, so I will not leave my own living ghost behind me, a cloud of bright mauve light.

Unlike Kyoto with its cherry blossom, there is no official aesthetic tradition of jacaranda viewing here. But I cannot be the only person to divert my car up past the long run of trees on Oxford Street to enjoy the way they bloom against the colonial sandstone wall of the barracks, or to look forward to the weeks when their glowing corridors rain purple on to the streets of Elizabeth Bay. There is an uncanny moment, which lasts only for a day or two, when the purple on the trees and the fallen flowers reaches equilibrium, and the trees appear, quite eerily, to cast their own reflections on the ground.

Japan's flowers are a delicate reminder of the transience of feelings, of life's bittersweetness. Our traditions are more robust. At Sydney University the blossoming of the bare tree in the quadrangle – like the cherry, the jacaranda flowers before it leafs – is a sign to lazy students that it is too late to study for their end-of-year exams. In my childhood, they were planted foolishly, or perhaps sadistically, beside public swimming pools, to the peril of the bare-footed, since the fallen flowers are home to drunken bees. They are often planted next to Illawarra flame trees, marking the streets of our suburbs with companion bursts of violent red and purple. Their unnerving fluorescence and feral vigour, for they are also able to seed themselves in bush and gardens, makes them less filled with gentle longing than Japan's blossom. They invoke something closer to a hallucinatory yearning. Their colours appear unreal, as if you have suddenly developed the ability to see ultra-violet. But there is more to this uncanny feeling. They are an introduced species, from Central America and Brazil, whose purity of colour does not really fit the dappled tones of our nature.

And so it shouldn't surprise us to hear that the same stories are told in Brisbane, of a hospital sending mothers of newborns home with jaca-randa seedlings, of a tree flowering in the university quadrangle a week before exams. These plants are so lovely that we can scarcely call them our own. While I always mourn them, it is almost a relief, a month before Christmas, when their ferny leaves crowd through, and the flowers brown and rot upon the ground.

The photograph has been taken on the Bondi to Bronte Beach Walk, at McKenzies Point: the Cadigal carving of a giant stingray. Its edges have been redrawn by the photographer in yellow light. Its shape is fulsome, organic. Three sharp gills are etched like comic worry lines beside each eye. As the sandstone promontory mottles in the dusk, the illuminated creature appears to float above it. A flat sea behind it to the south reflects the lights of low-rise Bronte. Photographer Peter Solness has captured the ray's spiritual force, a sense that it has willed itself into existence from out of the rock itself. Its bright outline casts a shadow, so that the enormous creature seems to hover beside the footpath, as if it has just lifted itself up from the sandy ocean floor and is now poised to swim off, into the still air.

There are no golfers on the Bondi Golf Course as I stand with Solness on the fairway, just below the cliff's edge. To the left of us, the sewage works emit a low hum, their brick ventilation chimney that rises in the middle of the course adding whiffs of sulphur to the stiff breeze. Nankeen kestrels bob and dip above the cliff's lip. 'Look at them – the great sandstone walls of Sydney', he says, as we step up to look out at bright water, and the layered stone that stretches, through the mist of sea spray, to the North Head in one direction, and all the way south to La Perouse.

This is where Solness shot two of the other photographs that have brought us here. In one, a mackerel sky still holds its blue, while the moon, below the horizon, casts a white path across the ocean. The lit-up outline of a shark glides across the cleft in the sandstone platform, which the dusk has turned mauve and pink. In the other, taken facing back toward Bondi, an illuminated lizard man stands, legs akimbo, his pointed organ large between them. There is an orange sunset behind him. Further down the rock he appears to have shed a large tail like a reptile's, or perhaps another penis. Water has gathered in a long depression in the stone beside him. In the daylight, I can see that the platform holds more carvings than Solness has illuminated in his pictures. There are some groupers, a dolphin, a sunfish and a whale. They overlap and enclose each other. There are probably many more beneath the fairways, Solness guesses, dug over in the 'gung-ho sixties' when the course was built.

To make his photographs, he uses a penlight and a long exposure. First – he shows me, repeating the movements – he takes the plastic cover off the tip of the penlight and attaches it to a long stick, which he has painted black. Then he sets off his camera on its tripod. Wearing black, he walks slowly around an image, and traces it freehand. This can take ten or fifteen minutes. Sometimes he will even allow himself to restore a part that is missing, as he has done here with the lizard man, whose skull ends abruptly at the fairway. He usually photographs at dusk, since he likes to capture the contrast between the glow of the city and the incandescent life of these carvings.

Rock art is notoriously difficult to photograph, he says; so much so that parks used to post signs encouraging visitors to wait for early morning or late afternoon for the best light. But some were not so patient, re-marking them with abrasive chalk, or filling them with sand. Here, in the 1960s, the Bondi council reworked the grooves of the lizard man with an angle grinder. The natural deterioration of the carvings is another problem. Once, initiated men would have returned regularly to refresh the etchings. With no Cadigal guardians left, current thinking is to let them fade away. Solness came up with this ingenious and respectful way of 'energising' the pictures several years ago. A special trick he developed, through experimenting, was to hold the stick at an angle, to make the ridges of the carvings cast their own shadows. This gives his images their haunting effect of reflection, of seeming to conjure themselves up out of the stone. It is a personal project for this tall man, who wants simply to remind people in the city of the presence of these ancient pictures. Where possible in the

Sydney area, he consults traditional custodians for permission to publish his photographs.

'I think of this process as "ghosting"', he says.

On 14 May 1927, thirty-year-old Joe Lynch, on the way to a party with friends, his pockets weighted with full beer bottles, disappeared from the Manly ferry into the harbour near Fort Denison. His body was never recovered. Lynch is the drowned man in Kenneth Slessor's elegiac poem to the harbour, 'Five Bells', which he wrote in 1939. As the poet looks out his window, and hears a warship's bells ring out over the water, he finds himself imagining the wild black-and-white artist, with whom he worked at *Smith's Weekly*, continuing his spectral life as an angry ghost beneath it. The young man who once raved about melons and Milton in boarding-house rooms, the poet tells us, is now a kind of elemental spirit of the harbour, 'gone even from the meaning of a name'. Joe, 'long dead', rages wordlessly against the passage of time and life above, from far below the sea's 'deep and dissolving verticals of light'.

Lynch was also the model for his brother Guy

Lynch's sculpture *Satyr*, now in the Sydney Botanic Gardens. Above the faun's monstrous body, Joe has been captured in rude life. His barfly's face is flushed beneath its horns, his eyes half-closed, as if he is wondering whether to recall some bibulous story, or start a fight. His thighs are matted and obscenely huge, the left barely able to cross over the right. Leaning back on his plinth, he hugs one knee with veiny arms.

Satyr caused a sensation when it was unveiled at the Art Gallery of New South Wales, three years before Joe's death. Critics described it as both a masterpiece and 'pagan work'. But Guy Lynch 'went to pieces' after Joe drowned, moving to London for almost a decade. He spent his last years on a poultry farm in the city's west, where he died in 1967. Ten years afterward, his wife had this bronze cast of the original made and placed in the Gardens by the Opera House gate. Now a symbol of Sydney's commingling of promise and death, Joe seems to bask luxuriously in the drench of morning sunlight.

This is all a temporary folly, his sardonic looks infer.

For all its vitality, Sydney is a haunted city. This is not a simple haunting, if hauntings can ever be thought of as straightforward. It is not just its human past that seems to well up. There is a sense that everything has an extra layer of reflection, of slip beneath the surface. Few other cities have such a compelling sense of being so temporary and yet so close to the eternal. None is so under the spell of natural beauty, but so addicted to the ugly as a kind of talisman against it. It would be hard to find another as vigorous and dreamy, as full of fecund life yet on the verge of decay.

Add to this the mysteriously porous nature of its sandstone, which means, after heavy rain, even when the air is still steaming, the ground is quickly grainy and dry. It is possible, in a single walk, to smell rotting fig and leaf mould, and the tea-like scent of eucalyptus leaves cooking on the sandy earth. In the middle of Sydney, one might walk by a tiny beach barely touched by occupation, where waves have dug their tiny holts into the cliff base, past the most modern and sleek of seaside pools, and around the 1816 marker of one of the colony's early roads; yet one will also have no inkling of how its Indigenous people lived here, or whether the same trees have always stood on the ridge above or replaced colonial buildings and encampments, erased before there was even time to register their existence. Sydney is not so much full of ghosts, as absences. It echoes.

In fact its physical presence is so strong, and so moody, that it is often hard for the human side to get a look-in. When it does, it has to compete with all this natural life – with mighty storms and great orange dusks that turn a velvety dark blue – without ancient human legends to help. For the language and stories of the Eora that made sense of the place are largely gone, and were ignored from the colony's beginnings. There is a sense in which Sydney is dogged by hauntedness itself, haunted philosophically; its ghostliness is almost depthless, as if – so quick and thorough has this forgetting been – there is a tremor in the bedrock of reality itself.

Then there is the sheer centrifugal nature of the city, which disperses itself along old convict roads to the towns of the Blue Mountains in the west and the satellite cities of the upper Hawkes-bury in the north, and through heath and sub-tropical rainforest to its southern suburban fringe, which now extends almost as far as Wollongong. Studded with remnant bush and national parks, crossed by rivers and gleaming ocean inlets, it is hard to pinpoint, exactly, where the city begins and ends. So much so, that it has been hard, at times, for its inhabitants to believe that they live in a 'real' metropolis.

But if there is no stopping point, no reasonable limit, on a city's imagination, then there is always the danger that it will find no traction at all. The more our writers have tried to come up with grand symbolic schemes, the more slippery the place becomes. No wonder we have such a liking for earthy stories of rot and corruption, which emphasise the city's textures, and return it to a fallible human scale. The story, for example, that the water that reaches our taps from the Warragamba Dam bears traces of cocaine and greyhound blood. Or the legend that there is gold in our sewers — which, as it turns out, is as true as it is perfectly metaphorical, because of Sydney's long pollution by heavy metals.

We know the names of only a small number of the original inhabitants of this place, the most familiar being Bennelong, after whom the point where the Opera House now stands is named. Kidnapped in 1789 at Manly Beach, with the senior Cadigal man Colebe (who would escape within a few weeks), he lived awkwardly between the colonists' world and his own; travelling in 1792 to England, where he was presented to King George the Third, he would return to find that during his absence his second wife Gooroobaroobooloo had left him for another man, Carroway. Then there is Barangaroo, Bennelong's first wife, who opposed his closeness to the colonists (a new high-rise development on the city's western edge will soon bear her name); and Arabanoo, kidnapped the year before Bennelong, who would die of smallpox in 1789 after helping care for and bury other victims of the epidemic that would kill almost half of his people. There is the girl Patyegarang, friend or companion of the young Lieutenant Dawes, who worked with him to make the only concerted study of the Eora language; among her companions, Wariwear, Balluderry, Boorong and Kurubin. There are the Dharug warrior Pemulwuy, who led dozens of raids in the 1790s on settlers on the Hawkesbury and Georges rivers; Willemering, who would spear Governor Phillip clean through the shoulder in a confusing encounter at Manly Beach in 1790; and Yadyer, Bullmayne, Dolmoik, Kurrul, and the brothers Bluitt and Potta, six old men who gave eyewitness accounts of Cook's landing to Samuel Bennett, the author of *The History of Australian Colonisation*.

The Eora, wrote convict artist Thomas Watling in 1793, were 'extremely fond of painting and often sit hours by me when at work'. 'Several rocks round us have *outre* figures engraven in them', he also noted 'and some of their utensils and weapons are curiously carved, considering the materials they have to work with...' One fantasises about what might have happened if Watling had shared his watercolours with these active, observant people; if they would have indicated the meaning of some of their 'outre' figures. But it is unlikely. Many would have been tied to sacred and secret stories, perhaps fully known only to the most senior members of the population themselves.

Besides, from the very beginning, relations with the Eora appeared to be characterised by an unwillingness on their part to engage with these strangers. After sending an angry delegation to Captain Cook's woodchoppers and waterers on the Botany Bay beach the day after their arrival, the Eora reportedly hid themselves in the bush. The trinkets the landing party had placed in their huts as 'payment' for stolen spears remained resolutely untouched; nor would they accept any other object, perhaps because the usual protocols of gift-giving had not been observed.

The Eora's strategic withdrawal in the first few days of the colony's official life seemed to establish an irrevocable pattern; and an awareness on the colonists' part of an elusive gap between language and place that still haunts the city. Cook, charged with making observations on the Indigenous inhabitants' way of life, had to resign himself to the fact that he would only be able to make them from the traces he found scattered across the sandy earth. He and the other mariners found themselves quite literally lost for words. Historian Maria Nugent observes that the expedition's journals, especially lengthy ones by Cook and the botanist Banks, are full of contradictory statements and amendments, crossings out, and new insertions. It is also possible to see this as the founding moment of our tendency to overburden the landscape itself with the expectation that it can somehow stand in for the enormity of what has been lost in the swift decimation of the Eora's language and culture.

Although other Aboriginal inhabitants would guide expeditions, and make other practical arrangements with the colonists, only Bennelong and Patyegarang seemed to have had any interest in genuine cultural exchange. Bennelong, who would give Governor Phillip one of his own five names, 'Woolarawarre', was a skilled diplomat: he brokered his people's co-operation in return for their freedom to move about town unmolested; he negotiated peace again when Willemering speared Phillip, who had had to flee down Manly beach with the six-foot shaft still protruding from his back; and, according to memoirist David Collins, discouraged other tribes from contact with the English in order to 'control the market' of gifts they exchanged. But words soon fail us again, for the only place we hear the voice of this senior Eora man who often lodged with Governor Phillip is his begging letter to the English Lord Sydney and his wife, dictated in 1796. 'Sir', it ends, 'send me you please some Handkerchiefs for pocket. you please Sir send me some shoes: two pair you please Sir.' Shunned by his own people, Bennelong would die in 1813, in James Squire's orchard at Kissing Point.

Other glimpses of the Eora are even more oblique. We know, for example, that Elizabeth Bay and Ultimo remained gathering places for ceremony into the nineteenth century; and Middle Harbour into the twentieth. Watkin Tench describes women body surfing on bark across the harbour, from Milsons Point to the city. Then, in 1789, the smallpox outbreak struck and killed almost half of the Eora. They did not vanish entirely: there are people living in Sydney today who claim their identity and country as Eora. Nor, by any means, were the Eora the only Aboriginal people in the greater Sydney area. (Even the meaning of the term 'Eora' is uncertain, appearing to be the word for 'people' that the harbourside Dharug used to refer to themselves. Other Dharug do not seem to have used it; nor did the clans of the three other language groups, the Dharawal, Gundungurra and Kurringgai.) But the epidemic was the beginning of the severing of Indigenous language and stories from this place.

Perhaps nothing more powerfully conveys this sense of a culture whose meaning would always exceed our grasp than Watkin Tench's account of a failed expedition along the Hawkesbury River. It is 1791, two years after the smallpox outbreak, and, with Aboriginal guides, the party is making hard work of it; or perhaps they're being deliberately misled. The men have come across a family with scars of the disease. They are desperate to meet more Indigenous people but seem destined for disappointment. As they continue over the coarse, sandy ground a filmic, eerie quality about this journey recalls the river scenes in Charles Laughton's 1955 film *Night of the Hunter*, when the boat in which the children sleep seems to be drawn through an enchanted forest by supernatural force.

'Traces of the natives appeared at every step', Tench writes:

> sometimes in their hunting-huts, which consist
> of nothing more than a large piece of bark, bent
> in the middle and open at both ends, exactly
> resembling two cards set up to form an acute
> angle; sometimes in marks on trees which they
> had climbed; or in squirrel-traps; or, which
> surprised us more, from being new, in decoys for
> the purpose of ensnaring birds. These are formed
> of underwood and reeds, long and narrow, shaped
> like a mound raised over a grave; with a small
> aperture at one end for admission of the prey;
> and a grate made of sticks at the other: the bird

enters at the aperture, seeing before him the light of the grate, between the bars of which, he vainly endeavours to thrust himself, until taken. Most of these decoys were full of feathers, chiefly those of quails, which shewed their utility. We also met with two old damaged canoes hauled up on the beach, which differed in no wise from those found on the sea coast.

But they see no more people, only these signs of past life. Is this the terrible evidence of plague, of the white men's own germs that have arrived in their vanguard and destroyed all before them? Or are the white men, like the birds caught in those delicate traps, being led into this maze of a landscape by their guides, as the Aboriginal people who have fled before them watch their every stumble? The landscape offers no answers.

Added to this obliqueness, until at least the late seventies archaeological remains of Aboriginal occupation were not much valued by the city, or protected. While thousands of carvings do still remain in the wider Sydney area, particularly in the Ku-ring-gai and Royal national parks, innumerable drawings in the inner-city have been ploughed under roadways, shopping centres, homes and office blocks. In her autobiography, *Fishing in the Styx*, Ruth Park recalls moving in the 1950s into a ramshackle old rectory in Neutral Bay where the tail of a sacred snake disappeared beneath the house and outside toilet. Meanwhile a handbook on Aboriginal rock carvings recounts the fate of six large groups during the building of a house in Point Piper — all destroyed, except for those depicting a kangaroo hunt, which were confined in the garage, and accessed by a purpose-built cover. When Peter Solness first related this story to me, I misheard it, imagining a trapdoor in a lounge room floor that could be hinged back during dinner to provide a talking point — a suggestive metaphor for the breezy disdain with which these works were once regarded. The majority of residents did not care.

In fact these traces were everywhere. Where the Opera House stands — which had previously been a tram depot with castellated ramparts, and before that Fort Macquarie, and before that Cattle Point where the first fleet's stock was penned, and before that again a small tidal island, Tubowghule — was a vast shell midden made by the casting away over thousands of years of empty oyster and mussel shells, which convict women then gathered to make lime for mortar, causing it also to be known for some time as Limeburners' Point. I have a strong sense-memory of being taken as a small child to a park in Balls Head on the lower north shore, where the soil beneath the swings was studded with particulate and limey fragments of shell. I took these for granted, assuming they were landfill, but realise now that they were probably from the area's vast number of middens, turned under by the construction of the playground. Still, this fragile past can be astonishingly tenacious. In the early 1990s, the tiniest of middens was uncovered by an archaeologist hired by developers in the foundations of a nineteenth-century terrace in Cumberland Street in The Rocks. Two thirds of a metre in diameter, and six centimetres deep, it contained eighty-two fragments of fish bone and eighteen species of shellfish. Dating it to 300 years before European settlement, when the area was known as Weerong, the archaeologist guessed that it was probably the remains of a single meal shared by a small group of people.

Yet the loss of the meaning of the Eora's language and stories, combined with this wide-scale destruction, has imparted a strange aura to the material world itself. Counterintuitively, this pervasive disappearance has led to ubiquity, to a pregnant presence. Some days each and every part of the harbour city can feel so richly and enigmatically charged, so secretive, that it seems more real than real. There are times, especially when the autumn mists blur the edges of the harbour, and the king tides rise, when one feels ghostly; when this place feels *sentient*, and thus more alive, than oneself.

An invisible creek also haunts Sydney. The freshwater Tank Stream used to emerge from swampland at present-day Hyde Park to form a channel between where Market and King streets now run, and then turn south toward the harbour. Rapidly exhausted and polluted by the colonists, it became a virtual sewer, gradually bricked over in the last decades of the nineteenth century and diverted under the blocky, paperweight-like buildings at the northern end of town. The original source of water for the colony, with sandstone reservoirs or 'tanks' cut into its sides, is now one of the city's stormwater drains. Yet this buried waterway is unquiet. In the AMP building, built in 1962 on pilings hammered deep into the mud, pumps must be used to clear the pulse and leach of water through its basement. Abbey's 'Tankstream bookshop' used to flood regularly. As recently as the 1990s, during the development of the General Post Office (GPO) in Martin Place into a luxury hotel, the path of the water had to be diverted from its concrete channel and through a pipe that runs across the ceiling of the building's underground ballroom.

In the seventies, that era of underground restaurants perfumed by the smell of stale breadsticks, Johnny Walker's Angus Steak Cave used to hunker satisfyingly into the earth just above where the Tank Stream turned, its dark tables and black banquettes (where my friends, grandchildren of the owners, would assiduously suck each tiny mustard spoon from the small pots, then replace them) emphasising its impressive sensation of immersion. Next door the odd curve of the Angel Arcade, where the City Recital Hall now stands, seemed like an extension of this dark subterranean passage; an impression fantastically maintained by the owner of its Opal Shop, who stood in a tiny niche among the stones, his long white beard combed out across his chest. He ran a lucky dip for children. Each of its brightly coloured paper boxes contained a fragment of these iridescent and veiny gems.

But the Tank Stream is only the best known of the thwarted waterways that continue to agitate across the city. The whole of metropolitan Sydney is built on the great bed of a prehistoric floodplain. Look at any piece of sandstone in situ, with its sloping ripple lines, and the high end of each line will point south, marking its ancient course toward the sea. The rock acts as a giant filter, so that after heavy rain the city's surface may dry quickly, but its soft cliffs and stairways continue to weep; it is hard to overestimate the impression those walls at the back of The Rocks and around Walsh Bay made on me as a child, with their mossy extrusions, like running snot. Even now, these tiny natural waterfalls thrill me.

Most of the demarcations between the city's postcodes also mark the courses of the ghost creeks that once rilled across the surface of its sandstone. Look at a map of our suburbs, and you are looking at a vanished topography of streams. These still long to be active, as owners of houses built in their vanquished beds soon find out when it rains, as the old watercourses rise to clog drains and well up through walls. In fact it would be difficult to find a city more permeated by water, since the harbour extends an extra two thirds of its length on the western side of the Harbour Bridge, and flows into the suburbs, through canals and mangrove-lined tidal creeks, as far as Parramatta. It is always a surprise to enter this almost secret western waterway, as still as a lagoon, with its quiet islands and gums and nineteenth-century stone bathing houses. It may be for this reason that Kenneth Slessor, who worked for most of his life as a journalist, and celebrated the city in his prose, described it as 'a kind of dispersed and vaguer Venice'.

It is unusual in a modern city of four million people to feel such a wild underlayer that so asserts its presence. Here the nature we have displaced enchants and bedevils us. Each dusk thousands of flying foxes rise from their camps in Cabramatta, Emu Plains, Yarramundi, Gordon and the Botanic Gardens, to land heavily in the fruiting trees of parks and suburban backyards. All night, at the height of the fruit season, dozens squabble in each giant fig tree, struggling along the branches like tiny amputees with the claws at the crooks of their wings. When they reach critical mass in the evenings, pouring up over the skyline, it can appear as if a huge fire is throwing up great pieces of dark ash. By day larrikin bands of bright white cockatoos call out in 'boys' voices', as Ruth Park so beautifully put it, dipping across busy traffic and joyfully shredding windowsills and trees. They are naturally playful, and like to swing upside down, like crazed morris dancers, from the fronds of palm trees. I have seen birds dip over busy Parramatta Road and once saw a pair nesting in a sandstone architrave of the Mitchell Library. Until recently, before a new housing development was pushed through, a flock of emus lived in the city's west, at the old army firing range at St Marys, on the remains of the ancient Cumberland Plain grassland. Further west, quolls raid chook pens on the edge of the Blue Mountains. 'It's like a jungle', an agoraphobic Irish friend staying with us remarked, woken by the dawn laughter of kookaburras and the screeches of headlong lorikeets, pulling their cries like bright shuttles through the air.

But that is not the half of it. Sydney houses are subject to invasions from mosquitoes, possums, huntsman spiders; midges, and crickets;

cockroaches of various sizes, which are especially irksome in summer when they take wing; and a seasonal influx of Christmas beetles, which bounce crazily around light bulbs in December. During the parties of my childhood, the cry of 'Redback!' – or, more urgently, 'Funnel web!' – would bring parents at a life-saving sprint from inner house to back yard. School playgrounds were sometimes infested by living black cow pats of hairy caterpillars, which reared their heads in frightening rhythm and were said to spit poison; the standard treatment for these wasp larvae was annihilation by boiling water, an execution my mother carried out only once – she was stricken by guilt thereafter.

Depending on the air currents from the Snowy Mountains, where bogong moths estivate, dark shoals of varying density clog the ventilation shafts of office buildings in October, and swarm around the lights at outdoor cricket matches, bringing after them huge flocks of seagulls. Long-beaked ibis, having arrived in the city from the far north in the seventies, root in inner-city garbage bins, white feathers brown with muck. Mynah birds steal fruit from the kitchens of apartments. Frogs pipe and chirr in gardens. Drains house colonies of micro-bats. Only this year I found a colony of spiny leaf-tailed geckoes in my mother's garage, which rattle and hiss when picked up. Added to this is an apparently eternal population of flies and mosquitoes, which breed in garden clippings and damp leaf mulch. 'Flies – black, blue, bumble and blow – mosquitoes, cockroaches, spiders, tarantulas, and even centipedes, annoy and terrify the new arrival', wrote memoirist Frank Fowler in 1859. 'The mosquito is a beast. It comes buzzing against your cheek, with a drowsy singsong whirr, fixes its suckers into the flesh, and bounds off with another song – a kind of *carmen triumphale…*' Recently, during a particularly vicious summer, I opened the fridge door to find a pair hovering, unslowed and in rude health.

The sheer abundance of Sydney can be Marquezian – its moulds, for example, brought on by the monsoonal January rains, which bloom on leather jackets, handbags and shoes left unwatched in cupboards. Only the other day a friend texted, exhilarated, to tell me she had seen three fairy penguins swimming by the sandstone wall at Darling Point. My partner, kayaking in the inner harbour, has seen a bull shark, fat and blunt, leap and somersault in the air before him. But abundance can also mask a long history of loss: the devastation, for example, of the city's quolls, bandicoots, koalas and grey nurse sharks.

Such staggering beauty and richness have always been the city's great consolations, even in the early days of settlement as the colony, waiting for supply ships, almost starved: 'went out with my Gun and Kild only one Parrot', lonely Lieutenant Ralph Clark wrote to his wife in 1788. And, he could not help adding, 'the[y] are the most beatifuless birds that I ever saw'. Even mosquito-plagued Frank Fowler was infatuated:

> evenings in Australia are singularly beautiful. I have often read a newspaper by the light of the moon. The stars are very white and large, and seem to drop pendulous from the blue, like silver lamps from a dome of calcite. I used to visit a house a long way out of Sydney, for the pleasure of being lighted home by the stars.

Further on in *Southern Lights and Shadows*, that great moon is still on his mind.

> I have looked from my little study windows sometimes at midnight, and seen the harbour so brightly argent with the moon, that it seemed as

though He had walked upon the sea, and left the glory of His footsteps on the water.

Then there is the daylight. Look at any photograph of the city, even the stricken lanes of turn-of-the-century Surry Hills or industrial Waterloo, and the light is still bush light, dappled, elusive, melded to incline and unevenness, in spite of the overlay of asphalt and brick. There is the sense, too, especially on humid days, that it comes not from the sky, but the ground, that it is some glowing emission of the sandy earth. Especially where there are any native trees present, the plants also seem radiant, with a slick coating of brightness. And at dusk, when the light is most like that of the bush, the landscape gives the illusion, as it does in the wild, of undergoing an almost spiritual transformation from harsh to soft.

When I moved into the city's inner west, to go to university, I was often struck on quiet days by the feeling that its streets of terraces had not been built from the ground up, but dug in; established in the remains of some older jungle city long since overgrown. Everywhere in Sydney, perhaps most intensely in its built-up parts, nature feels rebarbative, as if it keeps a certain raggedness in reserve. Perhaps the most charming instance of the unyielding quality of the natural landscape is the surprisingly modest Wentworth family tomb, on its small bush block, not far from their colonial mansion Vaucluse House at Parsley Bay. Walk behind this neat gothic chapel, your feet crunching on gum twigs and the cicadas thrumming, and you will find that its back has been raised to straddle an enormous, immoveable boulder.

When the southerly buster blows, or hot thermals brush across its suburban escarpments, there is a strong sense that the city still longs to return to bush, to shrug us off.

Sydney's unwieldy reach also spooks it. Yet one of its few unifying features is its gauche dispersal. Unlike Paris, it does not fall neatly into centre and périphérique. Instead, away from its small downtown, it loosely inhabits zones – north, south, east and west – but within these are more significant distinctions, like the Shire, the Hills, and upper and lower north shore. Then there is the question of how far its sprawl really extends. Does it incorporate dormitory 'suburbs' like Gosford to the north of the Hawkesbury River, and the hazy Blue Mountains to the west, where towns filled with economic refugees from the flatlands are strung out along the train line? One of the great thrills of living in Sydney is flying in to the airport at dusk, and looking down on the maze of new suburbs squeezed up against its national parks, before the plane banks over the older suburbs with their red roofs and factories wound about with golden water. So many of its features are cut about by remnant bush and rivers, that it is hard to work out what's what. Is that the Georges River, or the Hawkesbury? Are those the Bible-belt mansions at the back of Sylvania Waters in the south, or some new extension of the west?

But this dispersal has psychic consequences. The result is a dreaminess, a sense of pleasant unreality, a spectral feeling of sunny suspension as one drives the endless streets and roads – which can, if disturbed, turn hostile.

The truth is that we do not often look past the balmy light of our own separate villages. And when we do, we are just as likely to look much further, to a 'real' city somewhere else. To someone living in the north shore's bush suburbs, the artificial lakes and dry ovals of Penrith in the west are likely to be less familiar than London. If you live in one of the McMansions on the edges of Windsor where farms used to stretch on either side of the highway, the inner west with its narrow terraces and dog cafés can seem as foreign as Bali. In the recent Australian film *Cedar Boys*, the inner eastern suburbs are a fantasy as distant as Hollywood for the young Lebanese men from the south-west. Other parts of town are not even places that we bother to tell ourselves stories about; they are simply thought of collectively as 'the suburbs', just as we incuriously clump the city's various micro-climates together as 'the bush'. These places only snap briefly into individual focus when there has been some terrible rape or road rage death or ethnic conflict.

It is not as if the city centre itself offers much in the way of an alternative, lacking the cultural and historical weight to make it a strong focus. Recent arrivals from overseas and interstate often report undergoing the rite of passage of heading into town to see what's on, and finding nothing doing. Especially in the last few decades, Sydney's chief amusements, eating out and drinking, have tended to cluster themselves in its inner suburbs. There is likely to be more life on a Saturday night in the restaurants and clubs of Burwood or Marrickville, or downtown Parramatta, than the city's main streets. Yet even when it was a thriving centre of hotels, grillrooms and clubs in the 1950s, you could hear this suspicion – that we are not quite a real city – in Slessor's comparison of Sydney to Venice. It is like a European city, but not quite – too vague, too dispersed. That sense of something missing is there, too, in Guy Lynch's embodiment of Sydney's bohemian spirit in his *Satyr*, the figure of a Greek demigod poised with his back to the Opera House and harbour. The models for a real city, and what a city could be, came here from the northern hemisphere, from places like Paris; and to find a symbolic language for the wilder Sydney they were part of, Lynch and his circle embraced the mythological creatures of another soil, and other forests.

Because we did not value our Indigenous history, our myths had to come from somewhere else to give us psychic grounding. The remains of our settlement history were not worth much either, so our early buildings, too, from barracks to mansions, went under the wrecking ball. In my earliest memories of the city, The Rocks were slated for destruction – a fate they were spared by the green bans – with protest notices on bed sheets stretched across the terrace verandas of the Cumberland Street squats. Even Elizabeth Bay House at the back of Kings Cross, part of the early Macleay estate, languished as an artists' doss-house until late last century. In an exhibition there I once glimpsed a delightful Donald Friend watercolour from the 1940s of a harlequin-costumed resident sliding down the spiral banister of its central staircase.

This is not to say that one did not dress up to go 'into town' until well into the eighties. And it is not to say that Sydney did not have a sense of being, in some way, a metropolis, especially at the beginning of last century, when street photographers would capture the women in our family in full sail down Martin Place, in seamed stockings and lead crystal beads. Living in twenties and thirties Kings Cross, with its cosmopolitan population and 'hasty tasty' cafés, Slessor would celebrate its neon-washed apartments, filled with the smell of sausages and the sound of trombones being practised. Even in the 1960s, he could enjoy its vestigial flamboyance. But there was nevertheless that sense of real life being led, somehow, elsewhere, most probably in England. And, in that decade, almost an entire generation of young artists would set sail.

This same niggling insecurity about whether Sydney is truly a city may drive its residents to consume its pleasures so enthusiastically as internal tourists. For you would be hard-pressed to find another population so addicted to those kinds of tourist treats usually reserved for outsiders: the food courts and shopping malls of Darling Harbour; the Bridge Climb, a popular gift for anniversaries and birthdays; and open-air concerts in its parks. It is Sydney residents who will be found flying by sea-plane to Berowra Waters for lunch, doing its famous beach walks, or departing their harbourside wedding by water taxi. Treating the city like a giant resort, we are extraordinarily addicted to driving across town or down the coast to surf after work, taking up the new opportunity to camp at the old naval yards of Cockatoo Island, or trekking to distant suburbs on 'food safaris' to find new restaurants or exotic cuts of meat.

Yet behind this aggressive joy, perhaps, is also a melancholy motivation. If Sydney will not conform to our ideas of a city, maybe, through extravagant use, we can force the point. This may be why we over-celebrate our harbour. It is our one unifying symbol; the thing we hope can draw together all its different strands.

In 'Five Bells' Kenneth Slessor set out to do exactly this: to write an epic poem drawing into the harbour all of Sydney's exotic rot and ancientness and vigour. On one level 'Five Bells' is an elegy to brightly burning youth, to drowned Joe, of 'gaunt chin and pricked eye', whose bones have been 'long shoved away, and sucked away, in mud'. Looking out across the moonlit harbour, the older poet remembers the young artist, buttons missing off his coat, playing the fiddle and raving to his friends about 'blowing up the world', in Darlinghurst flats by the 'spent aquarium-flare of penny gaslight on pink wallpaper'. But the poem's real power lies in the way it puts its finger on the gut sense felt by anyone who has spent some time in this city, that there is a kind of troubled sadness within the beauty of the harbour, a longing so strong it almost seems to pulse and glow. It is for this reason that the poem has such a hold on the city's imagination, and continues to inspire other artists, like John Olsen, whose amoeba-like *Five Bells* hangs in the Art Gallery of New South Wales and whose huge blue mural, *Salute to Five Bells*, stretches around the foyer of the Sydney Opera

House; this mural seems not only like an underwater answer to the aerial perspective of Olsen's painting, but to turn its face towards the harbour outside like a strange phosphorescent echo.

From the very beginning of 'Five Bells' there is a feeling of uneasy reversal, that something is eerily out of whack. It opens by invoking the disconcertingly tender moment so familiar to Sydneysiders, when land and glassy sea seem to reach equilibrium. As night and water pour 'to one rip of darkness', the Southern Cross appears suspended in the water and the Harbour 'floats in air'. This feeling that land and water have melded into an uncanny mass is itself a reflection of the strange reversals of time in the poem's opening lines:

> Time that is moved by little fidget wheels
> Is not my time, the flood that does not flow.
> Between the double and the single bell
> Of a ship's hour, between a round of bells
> From the dark warship riding there below,
> I have lived many lives, and this one life
> Of Joe, long dead, who lives between five bells.

But beneath the harbour's glazed, almost moribund, stillness there is turmoil. Drowned Joe, 'long gone from the earth', haunts the harbour, but he is no melancholy apparition. The shocking thing about his ghost is its rage, as it rails wordlessly at life. 'Yet something's there', the narrator writes, 'yet something forms its lips/ And hits and cries against the ports of space/ Beating their sides to make its fury heard.' The decades lost beneath the 'turn of the midnight's water' have transformed Joe into a dark sea-thing with 'sea-pinks' in its teeth, unable to communicate, unable to rest, and filled with a primitive rage. The genius of Slessor's poem is that it summons up the epic, chthonic presence that seems to run far beneath the city itself. This 'something' can strike one at the oddest moments, catching the sharp smell of fern on the path down to Nielsen Park beach on a hot day, or watching storm clouds massing in the west like great sagging planets.

Yet, 'Five Bells' suggests, Sydney's hauntedness runs deeper still. Beneath it, there is an undertow of a more profound, even existential, kind of haunting, in which the harbour itself becomes an almost supernatural force that invades the city. In the poem's scheme of meltings and meldings, the harbour is already haunted before Joe even appears to haunt it. The waterway is immediately associated with a great damming of time, the poet's time,

the 'flood that does not flow'. It is already beyond
everyday time, which is 'moved by little fidget
wheels'. And Joe too, it seems, was already half-
dead, a half-ghost, before he fell from the ferry,
'living backward' so each moment of his blazing
life he was also creeping 'closer to the breast', and
to his father, a graveyard mason, whose work in
turn rested on 'a thousand men/ Staked bone to
bone, in quiet astonishment.' In this kind of infinite regress, it is hard to know where the haunting
starts, or even if it is a haunting, for there is no
time for Joe to step out of, no beginning or end
to this moment. And so, from the poem's outset,
Slessor is exploring the idea that time in the harbour city is put out of joint by the eternal. Because
time is bottomless, it seems to turn in on itself,
to be both infinite and instant. The poet may be
living 'a thousand lives', but these occur within the
space of five bells. In fact the whole of 'Five Bells'
is a kind of incantatory dream: dark, fathomless
and unanchored.

Because he is writing from within an abyss, the
poet finds he is unable to dig down to find any
meaning for Joe's death. He might summon up
the young man's 'raging tales/ Of Irish kings and
English perfidy', and the 'journal with a sawn-off

lock' that he left behind him in an attic room, but all these things amount to in his mind is the fact that 'someone who had been living now was dead'. In the same way, in this vacuum, Joe's ghost itself is unable to communicate, to even put together a single sentence that might redeem him from the waves that ride over him. All the poet is left with, in the end, is the sound of five bells, 'coldly ringing out' and the dumb beauty of the view from his window, as he looks

> At waves with diamond quills and combs of light
> That arched their mackerel-backs and smacked
>   the sand
> In the moon's drench, that straight enormous glaze,
> And ships far off asleep, and Harbour-buoys
> Tossing their fireballs wearily each to each

And so we return to business as usual, to the cliché that Sydney's loveliness trumps everything else, and extinguishes our intellectual efforts. Even our greatest poet seems to be left admiring his harbour view. But the genius of this poem is to tell a story that casts our materialism in an entirely different light, as almost a philosophical pursuit in itself. It insists on eternal shadows dogging Sydney's beauty, on some principle of distortion or extra reflection. It recasts any expression of this place as inadequate, as plagued by longing.

For these same reasons Arthur Stace, the 'eternity man', has become the city's other loved guiding spirit. Almost illiterate Stace wandered the streets by night for nearly forty years after an evangelistic conversion in the 1930s, chalking the word 'Eternity' on Sydney's pavements. Writing the same word over and over, in beautiful copper-plate, in the most ephemeral of mediums, he conjured a profound sense of mortality that seemed to manifest itself on the footpaths, along with the threat of damnation. This was also a kind of poetry, a meditation, on the city's combination of the infinite and fragile. And so it was a perfect end to the millennium fireworks in 1999, when his 'Eternity' wrote itself across the Harbour Bridge in red, blazing letters on the stroke of midnight. For once the city was almost united, cheering this as the happiest of choices, even if we did not quite stop to analyse it. It would be hard to find something more perfectly symbolic of the way the city's strange reflections twist time than the joining of two millennia by a temporary 'Eternity' made of gaudy fire.

No wonder Sydney, in the face of its implacable beauty, has such an attachment to the feral, undisciplined and harsh. Slessor's comparison of Sydney to Venice also applies here. For just as that city has a long history of countering the anaesthetic torpor of its lagoon with secret orgies, we have an enduring love for the tawdry and eccentric. Our indulgences may be given even more of an edge by the fact that our built history has been so brief in the face of a natural decay so always present and advanced. This affection for the down-at-heel and the mad-eyed was the other side of Slessor. He celebrated the city's mix of the grubby and mythic in his writing as a journalist at *Smith's Weekly*; and in his book of beautifully tossed-off light verse, *Darlinghurst Nights*, illustrated by the midget artist Virgil Reilly, who specialised in drawing exquisite flappers. For Slessor, the city's heart lay in Kings Cross, with its fried potato fumes and 'choker's lanes', that neon-lit place 'where peculiar ladies nod', just up the hill from his Elizabeth Bay apartment.

For seven years I walked every day past this mock-Tudor building in the curve of Billyard

Avenue, tucked in behind the white mission-style 'Del Rio' apartments — and almost every time I would remember his claim that he'd looked out his window one moonlit night and seen that someone was throwing dinner plates out over the water and taking pot-shots at them with a rifle.

For me, it is this wilder town, with its mix of deco primness and indiscipline, just intact in my childhood, which will always be my Sydney, the one I recognise and look for traces of still. I think of Slessor whenever I see one of the the white cockatoos from the Botanic Gardens pause to swing by its feet from the apex of the tarted-up Woolloomooloo Bay finger wharf, and shriek *faark, faark!* at the valet parking attendants below. Or when I pass the trannie in demure white court shoes on Darlinghurst Road, with a beer gut the size of a bar fridge in a modest button-down frock, who groans like a circus strong-man. I used to think of Slessor too, when I saw the one-eyed photographer with the ratty hairpiece ply her ancient Polaroid in the restaurants of Potts Point, before she died in an apartment fire. I have even found myself writing a story about Slessor, notoriously fastidious and deserted by his muse in older age — in my story he takes a young poet to see the old grotto of

Elizabeth Bay House, squeezed between the units, as a sign of an optimism that has passed.

But perhaps the most lovely monument to Sydney's indiscipline is its smallest. At the Fitzroy Gardens in Kings Cross, where the mansion 'Maramanah' stood until the sixties, someone has mounted convict bricks that were dug up in the area on a wall in its remnant gardens. If you look closely at these bricks, with their identifying marks of hearts and spades, you will see the skittering, sharp-clawed footprints of a small dog. It is possible to imagine the chaotic scene that sunny day, the bricks drying on the busy roadway, the idle dog following its nose across the clay before it set.

Paw-prints on the rim of eternity: I am sure the thought would have warmed even Slessor's flinty heart.

It may seem obvious today that this ghostly absence, which throws even time itself out of whack, is the lost world of the Eora. You watch the fidget wheels of Slessor's 'Five Bells' spinning, as the poet tries, with young, fiery ambition, to find a myth big enough to act as the counter-weight of loss. You can see this too in Guy Lynch's *Satyr*: the sculptor summons up a Greek demigod to try to give substance in this still-new city to his bohemian generation. This is by no means to project a modern sensibility into the past, for the loss was certainly already felt at the twentieth century's beginning. In the first pages of her harbour novel *Waterway*, which she began the year before Slessor published 'Five Bells', Eleanor Dark points out that the 'headlands were not Blues Point and Potts Point, Longnose Point and Slaughter-house Point. They were Warringarea and Yarranabbe, Yeroulbine and Tarrah'.

There are still places in the city of such forbidding gloominess, around the dull valleys of Northbridge, for example, or the cliffs of Killarney Heights that push drily down to Middle Harbour, or the scrub on either side of Seaforth's Wakehurst Parkway, that one wonders if they were used for secret business. 'Gone even from the meaning of a name', like Joe Lynch, they can say little more than, *Keep out*. Their silence deafens. It makes everything insubstantial, yet gives it an extra shadow.

Yet I doubt the Eora even entered Slessor's head

as he forged his epic poem. Instead, it endures because it so precisely renders the city's symptoms. It rides Sydney's wild undertow. It clutches at, and magnifies, a restless sense of not being able to feel entirely at home in or out of the water.

And, unintentionally, 'Five Bells' summons up yet another mysterious reflection, which, in keeping with the strange time-slips of Slessor's poem, pre-exists it. And that is the poem 'Sung on seeing Pelicans', in Lieutenant Dawes's notebooks, the only verse of the Eora's to have been recorded:

> *No-tu-lu-bru-law-law no-tie*
>
> *Gnoo-roo-me, ta-tie, na-tie, na-tie*
>
> *No-tu-lu-bru-law-law ne-lie*
>
> *Gnoo-roo-me, ta-tie, na-tie, no-tie*
>
> *Tar-rah-wow, ta-rah-wow.*

These untranslated words, in turn, make ghosts of us, no matter how brightly we blaze in this city. Forming their lips against the portals of space, they well up unanswered in every corner of the city, perhaps when it is at its most sleek and modern.

Dreaming

'Got up early this morning and Sent all the convicts on Shore', young, stitched-up Lieutenant
Ralph Clark recorded in his diary, 'except them
that were sick — thank God that they are all out
of the Ship hope in God that I will have nothing
to doe with them any more...' Since leaving England with the First Fleet he had been nauseated
and tormented by the wickedness of the women
convicts in his charge on the *Friendship*. Plagued by
seasickness and longing, he had contemptuously
noted their difference to his beloved wife, Betsey
Alicia, for whom he wrote these copious entries,
and whose portrait he took from its bag around
his neck, and kissed, each Sunday.

Clark's regret at leaving her and his young son
behind took shape in relentless dreams: of Alicia

giving him a piece of gold, or a dead louse, but mostly of 'being with' her in their bed. He might have been less tormented if his commanding officer had granted his request to spend his last night with Alicia on shore; or if he let himself drink something more soporific at bedtime than his usual lemonade. Often his 'dear and tender' Alicia visited his sleep in strange premonitions: she seemed to appear in the barracks, crying in her 'old Black Silk gown'; he brought home a new drum for his son and she told him he was dead; or she walked in a 'Strange Place' in the rain. At other times his dreams returned him to his domestic routine: visiting his Aunt Hawkings; dining at the Crab Tree Turnpike house; and, very frequently, spending time with his best friend Kempster, taking him in his arms and kissing him, or walking with him to a mill, before he disappeared. During his daylight hours, he tortured himself more. Reading a play about Lady Jane Gray, he was moved to observe of the young queen, 'She did love her husband but not half So much as I love my adorable Alicia — god only knows how much that I love her From the bottom of my Soul...' Even if she was on board, and seasick, he wrote, 'I should be able to have You in my arms and attend You...'

At last, after days of running along the shore of Botany Bay, and seeing fires lit by its Aboriginal inhabitants, Clark landed at Port Jackson, where 'The Tents look a prety amonst the Trees...' In the chaos of disembarking he had managed to get all of his belongings except for a box of shot, including his two hens and a pig, and was sharing a tent with his shipmate Tom Davy. But just three days later, on 31 January 1788, on a night of terrible storms when he had had to scramble to fix the slack tent poles in nothing but his shirt, he was dreaming again of 'You my dear Sweet woman and that I was in bed with you and that I dreamt also that I was very Angry with You and that I wanted to run Kempster throu for a Breach of Friendship...' The wording is ambiguous. Did Clark's imagination cross the line and make him see his wife 'with' Kempster? Perhaps it was the heat and thunder, or receiving no letter from her en route.

This is the first dream, to my knowledge, to be recorded in the city.

Clark was never to rise in the naval ranks, and would finally give in to temptation three years later, in 1791, fathering a child — named, significantly, Alicia — with one of the detested convict women on Norfolk Island. And although he was reunited with his wife the next year, she would die in 1794 giving birth to their stillborn child – though Clark might never have known this: he died around the same time in Haiti of yellow fever, twelve days before their nine-year-old son, a midshipman on the same boat.

But Clark leaves a psychic mark on the city as important as his cordial, if unproductive, visits to the local Indigenous groups, or his name on the island where he tended his tiny private garden. Sleepy Clark Island, with its raggy little clump of trees at one edge, can be seen as a monument to the city's dreamers. This is especially the case at night, when the water is flat and you have the illusion that you could walk from McKell Point to Taronga Zoo, between which it marks the mid-point, while the Manly ferry, its lights reflected in the harbour, appears to propel itself along on little wheels of fire. It reminds us that Sydney's great beauty, and its nearness to the eternal, have always attracted the visionary; and that the dreams it prompts are often extravagant, perverse and febrile. For this same reason, because the environment they grow in is so harsh, they can turn quickly to nightmares.

Perhaps I am overly sensitised because I grew up in the city's romantic period, in the late sixties and seventies, squeezed between its faded golden age and destruction. If I am driving in the car along the Cahill Expressway on a rainy evening, and see Luna Park's fairy-lit cupolas and grinning face suspended between the grey of air and water, I am struck to the heart, taken back to the primal scene of my childhood.

An only child, I spent the first seven years of my life in a unit in McMahons Point, listening to the gasps and plunging screams of the passengers on the Big Dipper. Luna Park, opposite, was my playground. My mother took me on the small ferry to play in the candy-coloured tubes and 1930s-style moving walkways of Coney Island's Funnyland. There was a hall of mirrors, and a tiny elephant in a case that squirted water at the glass when you stood on a secret panel. There was a polished, flat wooden button that spun children from its surface, which I loved. But my memory returns most often to the River Caves, where small boats bumped along underwater tracks through gelato-lit landscapes of mermaids in coral grottoes, flamingos by waterfalls, and a sailing boat wrecked on arctic ice.

Sickly purples, greens and pinks also played through the dandelion spray of the El Alamein Fountain in Kings Cross. There was a cinema at this time in the old Metro theatre in Orwell Street. After we had seen *The Wizard of Oz* late one afternoon, my parents took me — past the strip clubs with their large glossy photographs of naked women — to the waxworks, situated in the old Springfield Mall. Two displays affected me deeply: a body impaled upon a giant 'Algerian hook'; and the re-creation of a shark attack at Balmoral Beach, the shark hauled by lifesavers up onto the sand, still attached to its teenage victim's mangled leg.

Big fogs seemed more common then, perhaps because of the pollution. Often I would turn to see the ghost-outline of a container ship as it made its way beneath the Bridge, alerted by its mournful foghorn — a sound that still thrills me when I hear it from the apartment where I live now, although I have no view of the harbour. On the drive to my grandmother's flat in Darling Point, often only a dim shape from the north side, we would pass the rotting finger wharves of Woolloomooloo, where the peeling, grey military paint seemed like a denser concentration of the leaden water (the harbour was filthy then), and wind beneath the rising 'Lego' apartments on the Victoria Street cliff at Potts Point. The activist Juanita Nielsen's body was buried in the foundations, my father always said. These inner water suburbs were in a state of neglect, their low cottages and mock-Tudor flats slated for modern replacements. If we took the other route along Bourke Street, beneath the half-built Eastern Suburbs rail line, I would be worried almost to sickness by the word OBJECTIVISION, in descending and ascending capitals, which someone had sprayed onto one of the stanchions. The word repeated itself in my head; its psychedelic energy was disturbing. Like the mournful eyes of Dr Eckleburg in *The Great Gatsby*, it seemed to hold some message, to mark a mysterious threshold between the city's refurbishments and the freedoms of its dappled decay.

Lieutenant William Dawes is one of the city's first, and most likeable, dreamers. He also arrived with the First Fleet Marines in 1788, on the *Sirius*.

As surveyor and engineer, he constructed the batteries at the entrance to Sydney Cove, kept the settlement's chronometer in order, and laid out the government farm and the streets and allotments of Sydney and Parramatta. As a hobby he followed the weather, making his observations five times a day in a neat hand. Keenly interested in the area's geography, he led a party across the Nepean River into the foothills of the Blue Mountains; he later explored its upper reaches with Watkin Tench, who was to write the most lively and interesting accounts of life in the early colony. Most poignantly, Dawes was part of a long and unacknowledged tradition of Australian engineers and surveyors, like RH Mathews, who would become self-taught anthropologists, their intense and careful mapping of the land perhaps preparing them to find comradeship, and deep satisfaction, in Aboriginal stories and language.

Street grids and measurements were Dawes's day job, the stars and Eora language his nightwork. Almost as soon as he landed, he began to build an observatory near where the southern stanchions of the Harbour Bridge now stand. Supplied with instruments by the Board of Longitude, he was charged by the astronomer royal, Dr Nevil

Maskelyne, with watching for a comet expected later that year. Although the comet did not come, Dawes spent as much time as possible camped out, making his observations, to the point that colonist Elizabeth Macarthur described him famously and, one thinks, fondly as, 'so much engaged with the stars that to mortal eyes he is not always visible'. In this rare verbal portrait, Dawes appears as a dreamy, gentle man. That he was the closest friend of educated and gregarious Watkin Tench, who spent hours with him at this spot, also suggests he possessed a quiet charisma and focus. Certainly Dawes's curiosity, or a quality of kindly still-ness, must have allowed him to form a relation-ship of trust, the exact nature of which remains uncertain, with the teenage Patyegarang. In fact, a large number of Eora companions appear to have shared the bluff with Dawes; he names sixteen in his notebooks.

These 'language notebooks', which are now regarded as among the most precious of our colo-nial records, remained virtually unknown until they were discovered at the University of London in 1972. The softness of night can be felt every-where inside them. Like the stars, the Eora words Dawes recorded are fragments now of something grander, as suggestive and ungraspable as the far-off ice-light of other planets. From Patyegarang Dawes learned the words meaning 'snot' and 'hiccough' and 'the point of a spear'; but also more intriguingly intimate constructions such as 'to warm one's hand by the fire and then to squeeze gently the fingers of another person', 'we shall sleep separate', and to 'extinguish a candle'. Many other words – 'to embrace, to hug' and 'when will you be sick again' – seem to wear a night-time mantle. It is impossible to guess, beyond the fellowship that radiates from these pages, what dreams the Eora held for the transmission of their words to Dawes as they watched the stars together. (It is worth pausing here for a moment to consider how large the stars and planets loomed in the imagination of the colony. The search for the great Southern continent had only been secondary, after all, to Captain Cook's commission to observe the 1769 transit of Venus in Tahiti.)

But Dawes's notebooks are not dry grammars. Instead, as the academic Ross Gibson has noted, they became something more visionary, soon drifting away from Dawes's tables of nouns and verb declensions to record more complicated transactions. At one point in the notebooks, Patyegarang, or Patye as Dawes sometimes calls her, tells him that the Cammeraigal are fearful 'because of the guns'. At another, praising his ability to speak, she tells him he has a 'good mouth'. Other vignettes offer tantalising glimpses of lost moments: 'My friend, he sings about you'; 'My friend, let us (two) go and bathe'; 'I am very angry'; 'Take hold of my hand and help me up'.

Recently it has become possible to pull up Dawes's notebooks on the internet, and track through the tidy, browning pages in order, an activity which has all the drama of a gripping poem, as the imagination jumps in to fill the gaps. What is the story behind the phrase, 'Thou pinchedst'? Or 'You beat her while she was asleep'? One has to imagine, too, how close to the city's geological heart, to the raw edges of its harbour, Dawes must have felt as he watched the milky spread of the stars above him, or watched the morning mist hang above the water. Like so many of the city's visionaries who would follow, he opened himself up to this landscape, let it pour in; but, unlike so many others, he does not appear to have suffered any derangement, perhaps because he let it call to him in its own language. Scroll to the last page of his third notebook and you will find a kind of poem, each word on a separate line, which perfectly captures the future city's mix of the grossly material and stellar: 'the Penis, hair, Scrotum, Testicles, Moon'.

How differently the colonial moment might have turned out, if Dawes had not fallen foul of Captain Arthur Phillip. First, Phillip accused him of buying flour from a convict's ration – a serious breach of duty, with food in short supply, although Dawes claimed it was the convict's own earned property to sell. Then, in 1790, an Aboriginal man killed the governor's convict gamekeeper and Dawes was ordered to mount a punitive expedition, in which he was expected to execute some men on the spot, and capture others to be sent to Norfolk Island. He refused at first; and when he finally accepted, he made it known that he regretted being a part of the party – which subsequently failed to find its victims. When his three years of service in the navy ended, England approved his application for the position of engineer. But Phillip agreed to endorse it only if Dawes apologised for both instances, which he would not do. He sailed out at the end of 1791, later becoming governor of Sierra Leone, and working for the anti-slavery cause. In 1826, finding himself embarrassingly short of money, he would put in a claim, which Tench supported, for extra remuneration for his work as engineer and surveyor in New South Wales; the Colonial Office refused.

Dawes died in Antigua in 1836. His time with the stars and his friends had left few physical traces on the city. On 28 August 1795, John Crosley, astronomer with the HMS *Providence*, arrived in Sydney. Going on shore to the place where Dawes's observatory had been, he 'found nothing standing but the uprights which supported the roof and the pillar on which he placed his quadrants'.

Industry and sunshine: my childhood was cast in the textures of their combination, of old build-ings that still seemed to long for their past useful lives, and dreamy torpor. My parents were unusual in choosing to live in a unit in McMahons Point, overlooking what was still a working harbour, in the city's neglected inner zone. There were three active boatyards, and trains still moved along the goods line at the end of the bay; old homeless men camped in its arches. The parks and playgrounds were sun-struck and empty. I was aware of only three other children in this suburb of old cottages, boarding houses and units inhabited largely by single people. Most young families had made the exodus to the new suburbs, with their demonstration homes and sandy bush blocks marked out by surveyors' pegs. At the same time, industry had abandoned the edges of the inner harbour, or was on the verge of moving, to new factory areas like Ryde and the distant outer suburbs; which meant its power stations, soap factories, warehouses and docks were now great ruins, or at least, if still just working, graced by imminent decay. The city centre was also filled with buildings marked for demolition.

My father, an industrial graphic designer who worked from home with my mother, also kept an office in York Street. For the city was still the business centre, and still held onto the remnants of its cosmopolitan ambitions. Farmer's department store put on a yearly children's pantomime, and the brass chutes of the GPO stayed brightly polished. My parents kept a private box there, and a safe deposit in the basement of a nearby bank with an airless marble vestibule that smelled of wax. On special occasions, suburban families still dressed up and drove in to the revolving restaurants of the Summit, in Australia Square, and later of the new

Centrepoint Tower, with their giant butter carvings of swans and kangaroos. But the once-thriving clubs and coffee houses and theatres of my parents' courtship – the Trocadero, Cahill's, Rowe Street – were no longer. The great department stores at the city's southern end had also shut down, marked for replacement by office space, then in short supply. Anthony Hordern's, where it was once famously possible to buy both a tractor and a bridesmaid's dress, was now a white ruin of plaster wreaths and garlands that filled a whole block, like a giant version of Miss Havisham's wedding cake. Mark Foy's 'Piazza', where my agoraphobic grandmother had shamed my young father by succumbing to a bilious attack in the foyer, was barely holding on, its outside stairways crusted with pigeon guano. It was difficult to see the grimy cupolas of the Queen Victoria Building behind its hoardings; the grand building was destined at the time to become a car park. Go further, to the city's western edge, and almost the whole of Darling Harbour and Pyrmont were industrial ruins, places of empty quarries, marine administration buildings and Victorian bond stores; block-fronted workers' terraces with fume-black sandstone; and dingy churches and tangled railway tracks.

My father would often take me into town when he went in to check his mail, or visit the printeries at the southern end of The Rocks, around where the Shangri-La Hotel now stands. Parking beneath the Bridge, we would pass the terraces in Cumberland Street, occupied by squatters, whose protests against the area's planned demolition were painted on bed sheets stretched across the verandas. Then we would take the steps down terraced Essex Street, with its thought-provokingly green grass; the site, my father said of the colony's first hangings. If there was an iconic sign of the inner city's melancholy abandonment at this time it must surely have been the purulent fish tins, awash with stagnant rainwater, put out everywhere for the legions of stray cats. With what a pang of recognition, then, did I read the description in Ruth Park's *Companion Guide to Sydney* — still brilliant, and my constant friend on this journey — of 1972 Essex Street, as if, perhaps even passing us, she had captured another primal scene of my childhood. 'Nothing but sunlight and silence on this little-used road', she writes:

> Two trees grow where the gallows stood, one a
> palm as tall as a ship's mast. An old woman has

scrambled up somehow, and beside the palm
she scrapes a horrid skilly into a rusty lid. Her
pensioners await her – three wraiths of cats. She
takes us for disapproving cat-haters and plops
the last ort of fat down into the lid with huffy
defiance. The cats flatten down to feed.

Park observes to the woman that this is where
the gallows were. 'Dunno about that', she replies.
'Cruel swine. Always doing something to some-
body they were. No different now… Then it was
people. Now it's poor cats.'

In the cool docks of the printeries, where the
carthorses once shuffled from foot to foot, I
would play in the big bins of off-cuts that released
the feral smell of ink, while children called out in
the hidden yard of the convent school next door.

But slowly, new office blocks were going up at
the northern end of the city, around the base of
Observatory Hill; and in North Sydney. Miraculously, in the middle of this ugliness, the Opera
House was also rising; from our small balcony
we could see the stepped forecourt emerging. But
here, too, in sleepy McMahons Point, where pet
cockatoos sat on front gates and deadly nightshade
climbed the cliffs, new apartment buildings were

slowly replacing the old mansions at the harbour's edge. Harry Seidler's Blues Point Tower, whose long cold shadow I sometimes played in, was a sign of things to come; and, I was to discover years later when I studied law, the inspiration for a precedent-setting defamation case. Cartoonist Patrick Cook had drawn the 'Harry Seidler Retirement Park' as a grim rectangle; it had an upper slot into which a giant nurse inserted hospital meals on trays, while a workman removed waste from a lower. Seidler lost the case.

It seems of a piece with the times that one of my two playmates in the local park was suffering from lead poisoning, that sixties childhood disease. So too does my mother's fear of dead rats and broken glass on the slippery dip (for the city's empty parks attracted these attacks by the peculiar). The inner harbour suburbs, with all the grim beauty of their busy tugs and vast container lots and rusting fuel tanks, were also toxic. For years the factories, abattoirs and wood yards had been purging their waste into the harbour's still inner reaches; like a return of the repressed, this too reasserts itself in the city's present life. A layer of heavy metals lies locked into the sediment of the sea floor; 7000 tonnes of zinc, by one recent estimate, along with lead, cadmium, mercury and copper. This presented a problem as Sydney prepared for the 2000 Olympics. An architect friend, who visited the Homebush construction site, swore that he had seen a soft-drink can fizzing as it swiftly corroded in an apparently innocuous puddle. Since last year, families in Hunters Hill have been fighting for compensation after the NSW government failed to disclose that land it sold them had been used to smelt uranium into the luminous radium painted on the hands of fluorescent watches.

During my childhood a murky flotsam of orange peel, soft-drink cans, condoms and plastics was always visible, abutting any beach net or sand-stone seawall. Only in the last decade has it been possible to see the sand and green weeds through the cleaned-up water, and tiny schools of busy prawns. Nevertheless, in 2006, the government issued a warning to fishermen against eating any catch from the harbour.

My other playmate was a gentle white-blonde, blue-eyed girl, who used to wander down to the Lavender Bay park while her artist father painted his iconic harbour views from the veranda of their hillside mansion. We never met her parents, Brett and Wendy Whiteley, who would reverse down the long dead end in their Moke, call to Arkie to jump in the back seat, and roar away. But the sight of Whiteley, with his untamed mop of red curls, did not seem out of place in sixties McMahons Point. At the front of some of the other cottages, beneath the peppercorns, women in paint-covered kaftans would stand smoking as their cats stretched in the dusty sunlight of the driveways. One night, before I was born, someone had shot at my parents with an air rifle from one of the boarding houses. I did not feel the lack of other children. How could I, with the city my own exclusive possession? It is a feeling I have never quite outgrown.

In the late 1920s, from the rectory veranda of Christ Church, North Sydney, Reverend Frank Cash could see the huge shape of the Harbour Bridge as it rose, every part 'visible to the naked eye', at the other end of Lavender Bay. His three years studying metallurgy and mining in the School of Mines in Kalgoorlie, and ten years on the big mines of the Golden Mile, had sharpened his ability to appreciate this 'truly sacramental' wonder. It was to be the widest and tallest single-steel-arch bridge in the world, its almost forty thousand tonnes held together by six million rivets. Recognising it as a symbol of the 'imaginative power of man', Cash felt moved to write about it. His book, *Parables of the Sydney Harbour Bridge*, with its boldings, exclamations, and Biblical quotes, is one of the oddest love letters the city has inspired.

Construction on engineer John Bradfield's 1912 design did not begun until 1923, and the two sides of the arch would only finally come together in 1930. Until then the north shore had been dependent on ferries, vehicle ferries and private boats. Its bushier reaches were still the preserve of loners, fishermen in rough humpies, and small farm-holdings, many of which would remain into the sixties; this northern side of the harbour was dotted with grand homes, like the sandstone 'Hermitage' in Northbridge, whose owner, Arthur Tremlow, had to sail around the Spit and Middle Head to Circular Quay to reach his jewellery shop in the city. The north shore also had its fair share of bohemians, which may seem surprising now: like the alcoholic poet Christopher Brennan, a legend in the 1920s Cross, who would still make dishevelled pilgrimages to the family home on the northern beaches; and the Burley Griffins, who not long after bridge construction began would start work on Castlecrag, an elegant experiment in communal and environmentally sensitive living, where resident males favoured wavy hair and fuji-silk.

This joining of Dawes and Millers points would be the grandest gesture of Sydney's abundant Deco optimism, that period when it came closest to banishing any doubt that it might not be a lively metropolis with thronging trams, streamlined hotels, and new apartments with cocktail lifts connected to their basement restaurants.

Reverend Cash did not just watch the building from a distance. His proximity to the northern worksite meant that he could rush down to the water's edge to take a photograph when an informant rang him to let him know 'a fire wall was coming down in five minutes'. In the foreword to Cash's book, Lawrence Ennis, OBE, director of construction for the contractors of the bridge, describes the Reverend as 'a most constant visitor at the Bridge. The men and staff at the bridge all know him well and have nicknamed him the "'Mascot Padre".' Ennis added, perhaps with some ambiguity, that in seeking information Cash had shown 'a complete disregard of personal risk'. Cash would take 3500 photos in total. A persuasive, and apparently hard-to-resist, enthusiast, he also convinced the printer of *Parables* to make the 'blocks' of its many images for free.

In spite of Cash's title, it is difficult to work out exactly how the book functions as parable, a set of instructive stories. There is little argument or even narrative to be discerned among its enthusiasms, blurted statements, and italicised Biblical quotes set out, like poetry, in swathes of blank space. It is only towards the end of the book that Cash seems to move toward drawing any lessons from the Bridge, and then it is as a kind of embodiment of a holy mathematics: the top chord is 40 inches deep throughout, he writes, just as '40 marks the peak period of the life of Moses – 40 days and 40 nights'.

More surprisingly, he appears not to see this vast construction in more conventional Christian terms, as a human folly beside God's earth, which abideth forever; rather, it is seen as precisely the opposite, something that will outlast God-given nature. The Bridge, which 'commands the scientific interest of the whole civilized world', Cash claims, is 'a contrast in man's permanent artificial stone, to the passing life of the tree'. It is the Divine Pattern made steely flesh, through human skill. As the resident of a small antipodean city, Cash seems infatuated by the way the Bridge proves us worthy of international attention. And so he anticipates all the developers and tourist promoters of the future, intent on the world's approval. His Bridge is, as we might have said in the 1980s, truly 'world class'.

Even more striking is the reverend's fascination with destruction. In spite of his intentions to praise the growing structure, Cash is more exercised by the explosions and dismantlings that clear its way. For much of the early work on the Bridge was not about building, but demolition. These ructions in the city's fabric were huge. In order for the concrete and granite pylons to be put in place, great sections of Millers Point and The Rocks had to be levelled. So intent was the city on achieving this feat of engineering that it used a strong arm to evict struggling residents from their many terraces and shops; few received compensation or support, and some heartbreaking letters remain in the archives from people pleading for a few pounds' assistance. Yet rather oddly, for a minister whose congregation must have included some of these people, Cash seems unperturbed by the human cost. Instead, for page after page, he documents a suburb's disappearance. It is an aesthetic, and visceral, occupation; it is ecstatic.

Cash particularly loved to witness buildings in the very moment of vaporising – like the chimney top of Brisbane House, 'the big stones ... falling apart', he writes, '*in the air*'. Even whole streets, he records, 'completely vanished'; yet, miraculously, their '*demolishers never looked dirty*'. It was even more satisfying if an evaporating wall could be 'nicely *caught* by the camera'. He asks the viewer of his picture of a collapsing chimney to observe the '*sense of falling*'. In another sentence, laid out on its own and indented like poetry, he asks us to consider the workman: '*He went aloft, pipe in mouth*'. Many of the photographs in the book show masonry wrapped in the ghost-shape of its own dust, as if the very souls of brick and stone themselves have been caught in airy transubstantiation. Just as some romantics might look for the sublime in waterfalls, or storms, the reverend seems to get an ecstatic charge from these disintegrating buildings. *Parables of the Harbour Bridge* is a hallucinatory, vertiginous ode to ruin. Cash's fascination with the dirt-free nature of this process is revealing – as if the hand of God, rather than man, is banishing the city's troubling fecundity, in a literal clean sweep.

Perhaps Cash's intense enjoyment points to other, deeper fantasies of obliteration. His strange book seems to express a savage unconscious wish for the city to consume itself, to disappear in one dry puff. In this way he is truly a visionary, if inadvertent, poet of this most dialectical of cities. His book captures how everything in Sydney seems to contain its opposite. It may be that the counterforce to the city's staggering, almost infinite, natural blessings is the desire for their erasure. It may be that extreme beauty, especially one so unanchored, brings with it a countervailing wish for its destruction.

It is difficult, so long after Sydney opened itself up to the sunlight in the eighties, to convey how secretive, even illicit, its pleasures felt during my childhood. Layers and texture in which the imagination could find traction were the great gifts of its dim decay. It was precisely the lack of tenderness, or chic, surrounding those parts of the city that continued to function that gave them their enchantment. The old Strand Arcade, for example, had not yet been lovingly restored – this would occur,

after public pressure, in the wake of the 1976 fire
– but was a genteel throwback to the Victorian era.
At this time there was a passageway in its north
side into Woolworths next door, beside which a
man sat with his human weighing scales. With its
long shallow trays of trinkets, and smell of rubber
sandshoes mingling with the steam from counter
lunches, this store seemed another gateway back
to the less distant fifties, to that Protestant plainness lampooned so lovingly by the *Smith's Weekly*
cartoonist Emile Mercier, in his collections like
Sauce or Mustard and *Gravy Pie* with their depictions
of sweaty betting shops and garbage-strewn lanes,
into which the artist usually snuck a discarded tin
of gravy.

A little further down George Street, past the
Dymocks bookstore whose galleria level infelici-
tously combined a pet store and café, was a Chinese emporium with camphor-wood furniture on
the ground floor, and bargain tables upstairs piled
messily with makeup and wigs. It was here that I
learned to use chopsticks, from an ancient man
with a thin beard. For a long time I have had the
conviction that this store was the inspiration for
the mysterious emporium Peter Carey describes
in *Illywhacker*, in which his hero ends up in a cage,

performing as a human monkey. Beneath the Moreton Bay figs in Lang Park old 'Joe' the trolley man would push his worldly goods in a large trunk on wheels; into my teens he would grow more stooped, eventually supplementing his long coat with a crash helmet. On his death, a journalist would discover that he was Joseph Cindric, a refugee; and that the trolley did not contain poisonous snakes, as other journalists had speculated, but tools from his days as a shipwright and letters from a son in Europe with whom he had lost touch after the war.

I ate dinner with my parents in town as far back as I can remember, propped on cushions to reach table height: grilled gemfish at Flanagan's or schnitzel at a Hungarian restaurant with a sinister gypsy violinist, both in the dark underground proximity of the tank stream; or veal in green peppercorn sauce at the foxily mirrored Ambassador on Kent Street. My parents' favourite restaurant, from their courting days, was The Chalet, a kind of rococo hideaway at the top of a tapering corner building between two lanes, since disappeared, behind Customs House. Run by a Swiss woman, Madam Holderigger, whose chef famously refused to cook a steak well done, it shared its bathroom with the Windmill Adult Shop across the landing. (It only occurred to me recently to wonder if this shop's owner, with a charming sense of history, had named it not in some gesture to the spirit of the Moulin Rouge, but to the colonial windmills that once stood at the top of the nearby Rocks.)

Many of these places, I realise now, were removed from the street by stairways up and down, as if, for propriety's sake, some sort of obscuring veil, or interval of time, had to be put in place between outside and in. The result of the semi-hidden nature of restaurants and bars was that the imagination was forced to take a brief pause, to reconfigure itself from work to leisure. There was also a lovely sense about many of these venues of their having wormed their way into their buildings, like nests, or some other secretive form of animal inhabitation. This was partly the result of their having to make do with an older architecture that had seen little investment, or was being allowed to disintegrate until its destruction. But it was also an effect of Sydney's notorious lack of planning, its narrow roads grown crookedly, and buildings wedged into their declivities and corners, to create oddly random spaces. At the bend in the old-fashioned ridged escalators of the Menzies Arcade was one object of fascination for me – the dark Jungle Bar with its hanging plastic vines, next door to the Arthur Murray School of Dance – both places struck me as disturbingly libidinous. Another was the 747 Bar, in the depths of the Wynyard Station corridors, through whose smoky porthole windows one could see a full-scale model of an aeroplane's interior; I do not know if it is true, but I certainly imagined that the clientele, business men in shiny suits, were attended to by uniformed hostesses. Stairs led down to the Greek restaurants of Castlereagh Street, and up to the Mandolin Cinema, both genuine bohemian haunts; and up, again, behind the dripping hoardings and sandwich bars of the semi-derelict Queen Victoria Building, to its dim lending library. Most exciting, from my point of view, was the tiny roller-skating rink in the bowels of Anthony Hordern's.

Of course I was too young to feel keenly what was lost: that time when the city had been filled with residents, in units tucked between the office buildings and remnant houses; the great lacy hotels, like the Australia, with their secret back doors; or the cobblestoned laneway of pubs tucked in behind George Street (later replaced by Wynyard Station), which Kenneth Slessor wrote about in the *Daily Telegraph* in 1962 when the Victoria Hotel, the last, was being demolished. Here, in the twenties, he recorded every 'struggling writer, twopence-a-liner, licenced eccentric and general layabout' could enjoy a mutton chop or T-bone steak in the 'dim religious grillrooms' of Pfahlert's and the café Français. Even longer gone, swallowed by the past, were the tiny dens and licensed houses of The Rocks with their salty names, like the Black Dog and the Sheer Hulk. The great activity of Sydney's waterways had also passed: they had once been so busy, according to one of Ruth Park's informants, that workers in the coal tunnels that stretched beneath the harbour from Balmain as far as Vaucluse could hear ships' anchors bumping on the ocean floor above.

Yet I certainly felt the unfriendliness of the concrete stretches of the city between King Street and the Quay, which made long swathes worthy of Russian poet Yevgeny Yevtushenko's terse summation of Adelaide: 'a cafeteria built on a graveyard'. It seemed apt when convict tombstones turned up in building works in Jamieson Street, and that both Town Hall and Central stations had been built on cemeteries. But this oppressive emptiness was a spur to the imagination; the city's lack of respect for the past had the counterintuitive effect of enhancing it. What still clung to its tattered remains was texture: a sense of the hard lives that had rubbed against its edges. One could feel the traces of poverty, of hard labour, in the grim red brick railway viaducts around the back of the Glebe fish markets and Wentworth Park greyhound track. That feeling was also strongly tangible around upper George Street in The Rocks. The neglect of the Julian Ashton art school where my father had studied life drawing, Campbell's Warehouses and the still-functional Sailors' Home, preserved the grit of pinched circumstances and straitened pleasures. In Millers Point, the container wharves between its high terraces and the water were a marker of the area's continuing existence on the downside of opportunity. The almost empty corner of Sussex Street where the children from the Housing Commission homes played ball on the road, and the footpads where old men walked down to the water with fishing lines, were far more evocative of the past than the new development of Argyle Place with its craft shops. There was a sense that the city was still a pleasingly ambivalent place, brooding on what it had been and what it might become.

The dreamer who most captured the constrained allure of the city at this time, its *jolie-laide* poetry, is Patrick White. If you have grown up here you will recognise almost bodily in his novels the city's primal textures, of stubborn fecundity and inarticulate neglect. In them I find my own childhood eerily preserved: shady monstera deliciosas and bunya pines; an uncared-for harbour; cat women trundling trolleys of rank meat down pitilessly sun-lit back lanes; and Victorian terraces left to bake and rot.

White's childhood home, 'Lulworth', provided the model for both of the mansions in *Voss* and *The Vivisector* — Laura Trevelyan's, and that of the rich family into which Hurtle Duffield is adopted — and still stands beneath its ancient bunya pine, just up the road from my own apartment. Part of an ugly old-age home, its gates have been so battered by the passage of vehicles that one now reads, 'ULWORT'; though I suspect, were he still alive, this would have given the author some grim pleasure, since the building had been donated to the government by his houseproud mother Ruth, a towering figure of love and hatred in his life.

In one of life's strange ironies, White's Greek-Egyptian life partner Manoly Lascaris, whom the author met in Alexandria on war service in his thirties, would spend his last years here when he was no longer able to look after himself in the couple's home in Centennial Park. 'Imagine', a gay friend says with a shudder of horror, 'to travel all the way from Egypt to end your life in your partner's mother's house'. Each time I pass, I think of young Hurtle, ranging through the bush to Rushcutters Bay, where the apartments are now densely packed between Roslyn Gardens and the water.

In *Voss*, set in the colonial period, White catches the wonder of the eastern suburbs' early mansions, with their cool gardens and brightly lit drawing rooms, amid the humid protest of the bush. It is in one of these that Laura and the explorer Voss forge the strange spiritual connection that will last throughout his futile trek across the desert. But White's most intense channelling of the city is in *The Vivisector*, through the eyes of the artist Hurtle Duffield. At the turn of last century Hurtle is sold by his poor parents to a wealthy couple, who already have a deformed and sickly daughter, and live in one of the mansion estates of Elizabeth Bay. Hurtle has a monstrous talent for cold observation. As he grows up, he rejects his step-mother's cloying love and wealth, and is attracted instead to the ugly and misshapen. Over his long life and career, he will cut himself off from human warmth, determined both to shock, and to forge through the city's brittle pretensions to some truer plane. It is only when he finally comes to live with his sister, who has embraced the abject reality of her hump and become a carer for the neighbour-hood's stray cats in down-at-heel Paddington, that Hurtle finds a degree of contentment.

In its lazy beauty and incurious Englishness, this mid-century city seems indifferent to any spir-itual or artistic quest; but at the same time, some-thing about it irritates Hurtle's creative impulse. It is almost a fight to the death. Sydney, with its houses at dusk that look like 'unlit gas fires', and dumb dank harbour reaches, demands more from an artist than any other place. Yet if Hurtle can get past its gentility, he might come close to the struggle of creation itself. Like the ghost of Joe Lynch in 'Five Bells', Hurtle's brush with the city's eternal core makes him almost inhuman. Much of his work is demolition, the breaking down of landscape and people to expose their sad bedrock – like the prostitute Nell Lightfoot, who falls to her death from his bush camp on the north shore, and his sister Rhoda, whom he paints in all her deformity, after he has accidentally glimpsed her naked. As Hurtle tells one of the other characters, he is trying to find some formal order behind life's chaos. In his final paintings, he moves on from making distorted pictures of the city, to paintings of pure texture; as if he has finally connected with the ancient, dumb thing that Slessor sought, but at incalculable personal cost. In the end, Hurtle is not so distant from the Reverend Frank Cash, who found the beautiful city might only give up its visions through its, or his own, obliteration.

The Vivisector is especially gripping because it mirrors White's own struggle as a writer. Born and educated in England, but spending much of his childhood in Sydney, he would always see himself, with both despair and pride, as a cuckoo in the nest. Waging a complex war with the city, he loathed its smugness, fed off its social pretensions, courted its actors and socialites, and slammed down the portcullis on those who outlived their usefulness or failed to please him. Much of White's visionary genius appears to have lain in operating a mechanism of refusal, of keeping that genius within limits; deep down he seems to have had an instinctive sense that he might not have become as great a writer if he had stayed in Europe.

As a consequence of this ambiguous relationship with the city, he was particularly good at suggesting the perverse erotic spaces that Sydney's buttoned-down restraint opened up; and when I first read White this brute sensuality, twisted into strange shapes, is something I realised I had sensed everywhere, without knowing, in my childhood. When Hurtle stumbles upon the lonely grocer Cutbush masturbating in an Edgecliff park, he captures the polymorphous force of these spaces' grim emptiness. Yet the fact is that while so many of the characters in his novels face the same struggle to wrench a spiritual truth from the city, and though they might suffer horribly in the attempt, they do find an intense poetry in this apparently soulless place of grotesque social climbers and blazing jacaranda. Still, in the character of Hurtle, who revels in the cat piss and fried sausage lunches of his decaying terrace, White depicts trying to live as an artist in Sydney as a kind of perverse mortification. Isn't the course taken by his deformed sister, of humility and acceptance, the novel asks us, the more noble, less vain kind of art?

The constant simmering of love and rageful

loathing gives White's novels their great pull. In his later years, these feelings would harden in White himself into an almost parodic reflex. Each year he would rail against the invasion of the Centennial Park streets by the hordes parking to visit the Easter Show at the Royal Showground; no doubt the irritation was grist for more writing. He would delight in going shopping on the public bus, a forbidding old man in a beret with an ugly string bag. When he was finally awarded the Nobel Prize he refused to come downstairs that night to speak to the reporters, staying behind closed curtains until the morning with Manoly and the pugs.

White's duel with his city, its mix of the spiritual and mundane, would carry through to the end. His biographer David Marr records that White chose one of the most ordinary parts of Centennial Park for the scattering of his ashes, 'a scruffy stretch of water near the bench on which he used to rest in a clump of melaleucas ... heavy with lilies, with a scurf of plastic and broken glass along the bank'.

The bull-market of the 1980s, and the floating of the dollar, would ignite Sydney's great corporate redevelopment as a city. Yet even well into that decade, there was the sense of new things yet to be made out of its ruined glories, and old gems still to be discovered. When I lived in Glebe, in the middle of that decade, Blackwattle Bay was still fringed by industrial warehouses and abandoned goods trains filled with wheat. There were long streets of squats, while in Redfern and Stanmore students and housing collectives inhabited decaying houses in which the battered cedar hinges could be pulled back to reveal old ball rooms. New magazines operated from the warehouses at the back of Central, to which one climbed up dry splintered stairs. One of the 'witches' houses' in Johnston Street, Annandale, was rented by a group of a dozen young friends, who lived separately in each flag-stoned level, all the way up to its high tower; the separate servants' kitchen behind it had long since been burned down, most likely by developers.

The imagination could still play freely around these ruins. When I was at university, for example, the large abandoned blue-and-white ferry parked in Blackwattle Bay was supposed to be filled with squatters who shopped for groceries by boat and held the best parties in Sydney – although I never knew anyone who had been to one. Certainly, in the parties I did attend in houses at the back of Newtown or Camperdown, the old walls inside were often decorated, by students with time on their hands, with film projections or luminous cut-out stars. With a friend who was studying architecture then, I used to drive past the old silos and overgrown tram stations of the inner west, and fantasise about the flats or restaurants they might become. We had no idea that these refurbishments would become almost a cliché of the future, depriving such places of their memories of work, and their inner life.

But perhaps the most wonderful thing about Sydney during these years was the unauthorised uses neglect encouraged. Now the Bridge Climb is a paid tourist activity, but at my school in the early eighties, 'Bridging' was an unofficial midnight activity, conducted by climbing over the safety guards with torches – although I never had the courage to take part. The city still had some secrets left. My favourite story from that decade is one of friends who broke into the abandoned ICI lime factory at Pyrmont one night, a vast and rusting metal shed within a dark knot of trees.

The one who had been there before, slammed the door shut on the other, who when he turned on his torch, was confronted by the train carriages still on their tracks, and stacked with the hundreds of skeletons of cows and horses.

Of all Sydney's strange dreaming places, Luna Park must be the most iconic. Opened in 1935, a demonic smiling mouth forming its gate, the park is a gifted symbol of the city's eerie talent for combining dark with light. It is also, with its name, and constellations of bulbs throwing their reflections in the harbour, an unwittingly apt monument to the importance of the night sky in Sydney's history; a hypnotic fantasy on the importance for Dawes, and the many other star-charters and amateur astronomers who followed, of anchoring this place to the great map of the heavens.

But by the seventies it was struggling to return a profit. Sitting on prime real estate, Luna Park had narrowly missed being turned into a high-rise development, complete with heliport. In place of the more staid attractions like the Calypso and Flying Saucer, new management had begun to install thrill rides. But the park still languished. Then, in 1973, Margaret Fink, wife of the latest developer to take on the lease, had the idea of inviting pop artists to rejuvenate it. This was an inspired choice, for these artists, including Martin Sharp, Leigh Hobbs and Peter Kingston, were part of the new dreams flowering in the city's rot; Sharp had recently founded The Yellow House, a community of artists who had turned an old terrace on Macleay Street, in Kings Cross, into a living work of art.

The artists brought a new psychedelic energy to Luna Park, with bright colours and metal-flaking and murals quoting action comics. On the tower bases on either side of the laughing face they traced the stylised pop art letters HAHA, perhaps related to the OBJECTIVISION that haunted my childhood. On its back they painted an enormous mandala and eye. Yet by 1975, even as the artists were lovingly restoring the carousel, the threat of development still cast its shadow. New schemes were mooted, including a complex featuring a res-taurant designed by Harry Seidler, shaped like an ice-cream cone. While the state government pre-varicated, the park's lease expired, which meant that it could only plan week to week. At the same time, lack of profits forced it to operate year-round, without the usual winter hiatus to maintain its rides. In April 1979, a steel runner came loose on the Big Dipper and thirteen people were injured. But this was only a precursor to the events of 9 June, Cracker Night.

That night, as Sam Marshall's history of Luna Park recounts, there was a rail strike. Given the usual contribution to the area's soundscape of the north shore trains running back and forth overhead, this detail is particularly eerie. The only train running in the city was the park's ancient Ghost Train, created in 1937 from an earlier ride known as the Pretzel. Like many, I remember the ride as claustrophobic, dark and terrifying: a demonic maze in which round carriages jerked toward blind walls that suddenly opened onto further tracks. Screams and laughter played through the blackness. Usually three attendants worked it: the operator, a ticket collector, and an employee who patrolled the interior for any 'mischief'. (And, perhaps, reached out a hand to give riders a fright; the school playground was full of reports of scarily dressed figures who had leaped from the wings.) This night, there were only two staff, and both stayed out the front. When a fire started, it quickly consumed the building, which had no fire extinguishers and no emergency lighting, and spread to the River Caves next door. Both rides were destroyed. Sydney woke to learn that the bodies of six children and one adult had been found among the ashes. The park closed that day.

For Martin Sharp, the fire was the beginning of a continuing obsession. Haunted by the accident, he began work on the documentary film *Street of Dreams*, which occasionally turns up at film festivals or exhibitions as a work in progress. Also fixated on Tiny Tim, the artist began to intercut hours of footage he had shot of the singer and his ukelele at Luna Park, with material supporting developing conspiracy theories about the accident. For there were rumours – among them, that developers had paid off bikies to set the ride alight. In the film, Tiny Tim, his spectacularly plain face painted white beneath his ringlets, begins to blend nightmarishly with the park's leering gateway. As he sings falsetto among the joke mirrors of Coney Island, one is almost tempted to read him as a demonic spirit of place.

I have not seen the film since the early nineties, but one particular image has haunted me. It is a photograph of one of the boys, taken hours before he and his brother and father entered the ride for what must have been the most terrifying of deaths. He stands at Circular Quay where he will catch the ferry. Posed beside him is a man wearing a horned mask attached to a cow-hide cape that showed his bare torso. A muscular figure, he has his arm around the boy's shoulder, as if marking him for the devil's work.

Luna Park would eventually reopen after a decade of public lobbying in 1995. (Sharp and Peter Kingston helped design a memorial that incorporated a tree, and bench painted with the victims' names; but in the 2003 redevelopment, after the park had closed again, workmen uprooted the tree, and a bench was 'lost'.) For many Sydney residents the fire also marked the end of a more free and easy period in the city's history; a sweet pause in its march to destruction that was conjured up by the park's slogan 'Just for Fun'.

Living

Reverend William Branwhite Clarke was forty-one when he arrived in Sydney in 1839 with his wife and two surviving children. He saw at once that its

> coves are perfectly beautiful. The whole harbour looks like a lake, and the rocks on its banks, interspersed with shrubs and plants of curious foliage – here and there a dry solitary trunk rising up in grandeur.

'These are old trees', he added, 'and I would not cut them down'. It was a blessing, or a sign of Clarke's supple mind, that he felt such an instant connection with the landscape, because the Clarkes had only left England because they had to. Without contacts, Clarke could not progress in the church.

He was in financial trouble and suffering from rheumatic fever when he was offered a chaplaincy in New South Wales. But leaving Dorsetshire was agonising. 'My heart sickens at the thought of going so far from those I love. Vesuvius in eruption', he confided in his diary. The Clarkes had to leave his elderly mother, and the rectory where their daughter Emily had been born and died. These separations would be forever. As they rode through Plymouth in a storm, their five-year-old son Mordaunt called out, 'Look, Mama, the trees all go past us to bid us goodbye'.

Like so many immigrants who would follow them, the Clarkes had little chance to linger around the harbour, heading almost immediately on the steamer *Rapid* to the King's School at Parramatta, where Clarke was expected to act as both headmaster and minister to the towns of Castle Hill and Dural. Castle Hill is now a Sydney suburb, but was then an orchard town, surrounded by wild country. One morning, as Clarke delivered his sermon in the schoolhouse, a goanna walked down the aisle; he picked it up by the tail, settled it in a hollow log outside, and continued with the service. He was fascinated by the wildlife, sometimes capturing small animals for short periods to observe them. One tiny ring-tailed possum slept in his waistcoat throughout the day, a story sweetly reminiscent of the English painter Constable, who sketched so quietly in the countryside that field mice would creep into his pockets to doze.

Clarke was also expected to deliver the afternoon service at Dural, fifteen miles away. Soon he was making long journeys on horseback to his scattered parishioners through the untracked bush and stony gullies that now form part of the Ku-ring-gai National Park. Here he sometimes ran into Aboriginal people still living a tribal life. On these trips he carried his clerical robes and a specially made miniature communion set; a portable shower made from a large grey enamel coffee-pot; a fitted paint box; a writing set; a leather house-wife for clothing repairs; a tin box of small glass phials and wooden boxes for specimens; a large leather shoulder pouch; a theodolite and hydrometers; and a laboratory kit. His geological hammer hung from his saddle. Clarke was a man of enviable intellectual energy – a published poet and founder of a literary magazine in England, but also a fellow of the Geological Society of London, who had published on meteors, geology and zoology in the *Magazine of Natural History*. Like Reverend Cash, he understood the Sydney landscape as an expression of God's will, but Clarke had by far the broader mind. He believed God had given men two sources of knowledge: the Holy Book and the Book of Nature. 'Man should not concern himself with the incomprehensible – the Beginning', he thought, but should freely interpret the subsequent history of species revealed in the 'sermons in stones'. (He would defend Charles Darwin's theory of evolution when it was made known in 1866.) His papers on the sedimentary formation of New South Wales and its coal seams would convince the international scientific community how much older our continent was than Europe.

It is astonishing to think that within a year Clarke was heading off alone on geological trips through uncharted bush. Travelling toward Wollongong in 1840, he was invited by a local Aboriginal man, Bran Bran, or 'Frying Pan', to a big corroboree of coastal tribes. Bran Bran told him that the theme of the dance was 'the white men came to Sydney in ships and landed horses in the water'. In a hut at Jamberoo, he was able to note in his diary, that it had been twelve months to the day since he left England. 'The Evening was raining as this; I cried myself to sleep', he wrote. 'Tonight I sleep without crying.'

Only two centuries ago, even less, almost every suburb in Sydney was this wild. And each was filled with stories as powerful: of heartbreak and yearning; of accommodation and new love; even great spiritual satisfaction. Yet we do everything in our power to deny this. We insist that our suburbs are safe and controllable, even boring; we will even go as far as punishing anyone who tries to make them less dull. In another city, Clarke might have been remembered as a lesser Darwin. It is staggering that here he could be so thoroughly forgotten. In part, this is because we have never much liked our thinkers, except those like Slessor, who have managed to make the act somehow physical, to meld ideas with the slack air of this place. But our forgetfulness runs much deeper. It is wilful – almost perverse. Our suburbs are still our wild places, but we want them to be anaesthetised from any profound feeling.

Most of us live in suburbs, which means that part of each day will be taken up by train journeys through sandstone cuttings; walks through streets planted with council-issued bottlebrush; or long drives on old colonial roads that take in the city's striking mix of dark-brick Edwardians and fibro cottages and new McMansions. Many still exist in mad juxtaposition with nature. Waterfall, on the city's southern fringe, turns suddenly into open heath, a fire-scarred escarpment that stretches all the way to Mount Keira above Wollongong. At Sylvania Waters huge houses with boat-ramps overhang the Georges River, between boulders and old figs, while in Pittwater, on the north shore, the houses are two-storey seventies affairs, hunkered in remnant rainforest, with views of its sweetly sun-shot inlets. Even the least lovely of Sydney's flat outer-western suburbs has a view of the hazy shape of the Blue Mountains and perhaps a sense of the Cumberland Plain and the ancient foot pads of emus stretched out beneath its dry sports fields. Even the most domesticated, like Balmain or Ashfield, still have an untamed quality, a looseness, that comes from their raggedy palms overhanging the streets, and stands of peppercorns shining in the sun.

With such natural wonder comes risk: bush-fires and grassfires; savage hailstorms that leave thousands of houses unroofed. Only recently, lightning struck a home in well-heeled Castle Cove and burned it to the ground. And with such beauty comes ugliness. For every golden dusk, or street of flowering gums, there will be a factory or endless run of discount liquor barns, fast food joints and car yards.

Yet if we think of our suburbs as wild, it is usually in a social sense: riots in Macquarie Fields, race-related beatings in the Shire, Mafia hits on the north shore. These are usually, in our imagined map of Sydney, someone else's suburb. For Clarke's story also offers a glimpse into our suburbs' psychic underpinning. They still occupy the emotional ghost-shape of villages, or parishes. They are clannish. They keep their history, often at the peril of forgetting it, a secret apart from the city's broader life. They insist on regarding themselves as quiet, even eventless; as places where nothing out of the ordinary occurs, or ought to happen. If it does, they quickly seal over — but at a cost. As Clarke discovered, there is some absorbing power in this landscape, a variegated loveliness that can revive the heart. But it seems to hold an extra transformative power, a strange force of forgetting. Our suburbs feel weirdly tranquil, as if nothing but catastrophe can bring them back to life.

There was nothing romantic about Roseville Chase. Like most of the other houses in the street, ours was post-war red brick, its one individual touch a porthole window etched with two grazing fawns. In between Sunday drives to my father's family in Windsor, my parents had joined the families visiting the new land releases and model homes on weekends. In the end they settled for this more established suburb, just above the Roseville Bridge – largely for my sake, so that I could grow up away from the 'roughness' of the inner city. I didn't thank them for it. Instead I longed for the city's grit and salt air, until I could live there again as a student. Still, this was not quite the abject separation experienced by my partner, who came from England through the Heads at the same age. Friends met the family at the Overseas Terminal and drove them across the Harbour Bridge, whose mighty struts cast their shadows on the windows – and receded, until they finally reached Gosford, another hour away.

My suburb had no history. Or so it appeared, although there was a sandstone cottage with a sun-dial at the corner, and the remains of old sea baths among the mangroves and marina effluent at Echo Point. There had once been orchards, an older neighbour said, but it was impossible to work out where they might have been, as the soil here on the top of the hill was thin and balding, and knobs of sandstone pushed through the steep lawn like hide through a bad taxidermist's work. The house had only had one owner in the twenty years before us, a family of doctors. For some years medicine bottles would turn up in the back yard, although I always hoped for something older. I felt this lack of a past so keenly that I buried Tic Tac boxes filled with one-cent pieces in the hard earth by the side of the house, to 'discover' later and dig up.

I was marooned. No other child sang Gilbert and Sullivan with aging relatives who had performed with the D'Oyly Carte Opera, or was in love with Charlie Chaplin and had parents who would drive them across town for a festival of his films. We were unusual in having real paintings hanging in the house, the legacy of my father's art studies with Julian Ashton in the thirties. A number of these were nudes. (The models were hard-up, but dignified, my father said, and trying to survive in the Depression. There was an old sailor, and a woman who always left a ring of talcum powder where she sat.) 'Is that your mother?' my friend's thirteen-year-old brother asked, eyes crossing, when he saw one hanging in the hall. His parents forbade him from visiting again.

More than its lack of history, I disliked the suburb's conformity: its cream shag piles, its hushed and unused sitting rooms, its bland birthday sponge-cakes which were not the boiled fruitcakes with almond icing my parents bought. Or rather, I hated the fact that our failure to keep within these narrow limits was constant cause for remark. My classmates let me know how unusual I was. They followed me with questions. Why did you live in an apartment before? Why do your parents drive an old car? Is your father your grandfather? Why do you have wedding cake for your birthday?

Faced with the same coercive interrogation when he arrived with a strong Canadian accent at his north shore playground, one friend simply stopped speaking, until his second grade teachers feared he was retarded. Now a maths professor, he still finds the city's prying at difference unbearable. The suburbs were unstoppable in their drive to make everything the same. Almost every week another friend was beaten up on the two-hour bus trip from the northern beaches to our high school, until his father, hoping to boost his confidence, sent him to speech and drama classes; a near-fatal decision, as the luvvie's elocution they imparted guaranteed more beatings. How old are your parents? How much do they spend each week on groceries? my schoolmates asked. There were correct answers, but I did not have them. Another friend, whose first inklings that he might be gay manifested themselves in pointed shoes and a New Romantic haircut, was lambasted in front of the whole school by a teacher as 'peculiar'. It is worth noting that no class conflict prompted such ruthless pruning, for these suburbs were fairly uniform in income. Instead this interrogation was about policing the fanciful, and establishing pinched modes of behaviour.

In other suburbs across Sydney, the suburban war against difference played itself out in different ways. And so it had done, it seemed, for years. In his autobiographical novel, *Fairyland*, Sumner Locke Elliott recounts his gay hero's 1930s childhood. When he is twelve, his parents transplant him from harbourside Point Piper to suburban

Arncliffe. This may be a working-class suburb, rather than the comfortable middle, but the emphasis on conformity is shared. In a delicious outpouring of snobbery, Elliott writes, 'There was only one barefaced word for Arncliffe – common'.

It was the common denominator. It was the omnipresent Monday morning washing on every clothesline in every similar backyard, the unadventurousness of hydrangea and cosmos and lantana, the pretentiousness of plaster storks holding up bird-baths. It was the waxed fruit on the dining room table and the wedding photographs arranged on the piano and peoples' never-used hand-embroidered guest towels as pious as their teetotalism. It was the dull nasal voices expecting something new, the men all wearing collarless shirts but showing the collar stud at the Adam's apple, the women in curlers and carpet slippers wet-mopping the veranda tiles 'of a Saturday morning,' the plaintive twangy voices of the children. It was hearing for better or worse the steely pianolas playing 'Tip Toe Through the Tulips' and knowing that the Sunday roast with two vegetables was as certain as birth, marriage, and death and that there was nothing else to look forward to and, worse, their unheeding of their dreadfulness of not caring. It was the common bond of their commonplace assurances that held them together.

It is no longer fashionable to accuse others of vulgarity, and it may now make us squirm to hear it said so plainly. But it is worth noting that it took Elliott until 1990, when he was seventy-three, to publish his coming-out novel. So the message that he did not fit in had truly stuck. Read this, and you have the context for the fabulous life many gay men would forge for themselves in Sydney's inner city. And for anyone who has ever nursed a sense of exceptionalism in the face of Sydney's sub-urban regimes of discipline, Elliott's conclusion is thrilling. His hero had 'become quietly aware, per-haps ashamed, of his knowledge of growing secret antlers, possibly wings. That among these people he was a changeling.'

There *was* history in Roseville Chase, if only I had known it, but it was difficult to find. Perhaps the failure was my own. Yet, as my friend, historian

Martin Thomas, writes of his own childhood in conservative West Pennant Hills, the suburbs are wrapped in a numbing indifference.

Still at least some history seemed to have survived in Pennant Hills. The town had supposedly started as a signal station, Thomas writes, an important stop on the way to Old Government House at Parramatta; a flag would be raised here to show that the governor was fifteen miles away. His class went to this building on excursions. Yet when young Martin wondered if his own house, 'staring blankly at its neighbours' from its quarter-acre block, might have been part of the estate of 'flogging clergyman' Samuel Marsden (whose 1799 grant of a thousand acres grew into a vast five thousand by 1827), this was 'not the sort of information that anyone seemed to know...' Obviously his garden must have been something else before it was a garden. But, weirdly, after its residents had established the origin-story of its settlement, everything between that time and modern suburbia, when these houses were built, had vanished into thin air. In fact, Thomas would later discover that the story of the suburb's name was a furphy: it had actually been named after Sir Thomas Pennant, a naturalist friend of Sir Joseph Banks.

It was only while writing this book that I learned a little more about the area around Echo Point on dank Middle Harbour, below our house, in the shadow of the pylons of the Roseville Bridge. With its bush-fringed roads lacking foot-paths, pools surrounded by brushwood fences, and park marked by rusted signs warning of man-eating sharks, the area had always felt gloomy. It was a blank. The houses were newer than those on the hilltop where we lived, and isolated by high driveways; they looked temporary, or thought-lessly thrown together, on their partially cleared blocks. The bush was not an attraction for most owners, but something to be put up with for the sake of cheaper land. I would have walked only a couple of times with my friends on the isolated tracks that began at the noisy bridge underpass, where obscene graffiti was made more obscene by its weeping walls, before trailing along the water's edge and eventually joining the paths of Ku-ring-gai National Park. Yet here just a kilometre from my home, I have subsequently discovered, the naval surgeon John White had travelled with an exploring party in April of the colony's first year. Returning by boat, the party saw an old Abo-riginal man sitting on rocks by his canoe. They 'entertained him with dancing', combed his hair and beard, and showed him how to smoke a pipe. Afterward they gave him roasted oysters. And in 1791 a party of convicts had escaped, hoping to walk to China. They too, would have passed along this shore, once they realised they were beaten and turned back through Middle Harbour, picking their way among its mangrove roots and across the sticky mud that popped with crab-holes.

It was easy enough to imagine this early history. The huge St Andrews Cross spiders and the odd red-belly black snake were reminders of a time before settlement. But it was more of a surprise to discover that the new cul-de-sac estate across from Echo Point Park, where I used to play in the large Walker family's pool – a joke sign in the downstairs bathroom threatened the dozens of children not to wee in the water – had been, from the 1830s onwards, part of Bate's farm. This was 20 acres, according to local historian Gavin Souter, of 'partly cleared brush and fern with a freshwater creek, a hut, a few young orange, quince and peach trees, and a shell midden reminder of much earlier occupation'. The Bates would increase their orchard to 200 trees, including mulberries, for they also had an interest in silk (the second son

John would write a sixteen-page manual on silk-worms). Their grant had been made official in 1839, but the area had already been busy, before then, with the tiny huts of timber-getters and the gatherers of oyster shells that were used for lime. Yet by the time the Bate estate was sold in 1860, its working history was already disappearing from local memory. While describing the 'capital cottage residence of seven rooms, with numerous out-offices, and a beautiful full-bearing orchard and orangery of ten acres all cleared, fenced and in first-rate order', the mortgagee's advertisement emphasised its picturesque position:

> The romantic loveliness of the situation must be
> seen to be appreciated – being immediately on one
> of those delightful jutting headlands, surrounded
> by wild, bold, majestic scenery, softened by the still
> lake-like waters of Middle Harbour.

In other words, this area that had been filled with busy humans for many years was now seen, by an act of will, as empty bush.

There was more, I discovered. By 1892, the farm had been leased by a temperance group and turned into the Echo Farm Home for Male Inebriates, where its voluntary inmates bathed in the bay, prayed, and read scriptures; among them, the poet and short story writer, Henry Lawson. But a recent story was the most surprising. In 1951, Stefan and Genowefa Pietroszys, displaced persons from Lithuania, arrived in Sydney. Still terrified of the KGB, they made their way to a rock cave, probably one of the old Aboriginal rock shelters or 'gibber gunyahs', just downstream from the Roseville Bridge on the other side of Middle Harbour. For the next twenty-eight years they would live here on roots, berries, fish and rats. In 1979, an epic scene played itself out, unknown to me, below our house. Stefan walked out of the bush, and hailed two fishermen. One happened to be a German teacher, who understood Pietroszys when he called out, '*Meine Frau ist tot*'. They found Genowefa dead of arteriosclerosis on the couple's bed of timber and foam matting. Her address was given to the inquest as 'Cave under rock, Davidson Park, Killarney Heights'.

It says something for the suburbs' strange powers of emptying themselves out that a scene like this could have passed virtually unnoticed. And that was only thirty years ago. What had happened, earlier on, between the people who made the shell middens, and the timber-getters, and the Bates? Was it the absence of all these stories leading up to the strangely numb present that made this place a touch eerie – a little wild again?

No other major city is as penetrated by remnant wilderness as Sydney. One of its great pleasures is this variegated loveliness. Its dappling light, its legions of wattlebirds and currawongs threading the air with their bright song, the new crimson shoots at the top of its gums, grevillea shining like glass – all call to mind Gerard Manley Hopkins's poem 'Pied Beauty' in which he praises '[w]hatever is fickle, freckled… adazzle, dim'.

In his essay, 'The Light of LA', American writer Lawrence Weschler describes how tears jumped to his eyes on the US east coast, watching footage of the OJ Simpson car chase, when he recognised the steady light of his native Los Angeles. I had a similar tightness in my throat the other day, as I watched a scene in the Australian film *Bliss*, in which the hero, Harry, and a friend sit on a hospital veranda. We see nothing of the surrounds in this tight shot, but the light is unquestionably Sydney's: saturating, and warm, but also muted and inconstant. Here, in the heart of the inner suburbs, is the same unbowed bush light that you might find in the wilderness of the Blue Mountains. Its humid weight pins the characters to the wall behind, yet shifts with leafy shadows. This light provides a soft energy to early black-and-white photos of the city, and is still the source of a base-level joy, a deep relaxation, that imbues its daily life.

Yet Sydney's remnant bush is not wild; seen close-up, it is a half-and-half, semi-domesticated place, and it is this ambiguous quality that makes it unnerving. When we first moved to Roseville Chase there were bandicoots in the sandstone scrub on the high side of the street, which has since been cleared. Powerful owls sometimes swooped on the native mice in our neighbour's overgrown back yard, while possums and rainbow lorikeets, which had migrated to Sydney because of bushfires in the mountains, still line up at her railing. The Ku-ring-gai Chase National Park, nearby, stretched all the way to Pittwater, in the city's northern beaches. Yet, as children, we sensed that darker activity went on in this bush fringe. Most of it was human. Go down its unofficial footpads a little and you were sure to stumble on a campfire extinguished by piss, surrounded by smoked-down butts and pages torn from pornos. Further in it was a dumping ground for animals and stolen cars. A friend bushwalking with his father near Narrabeen came across an abandoned motorbike, covered in blood. He was not surprised. The bush was where bad things happened. When a ten-year-old classmate came to school and reported that her cousin had been 'raked' in leafy Castlecrag, the image puzzled and terrified us. It also captured a more amorphous, primal danger in the suburb's remnant scrub.

The 2001 film *Lantana* captures this sense of dense threat. It opens with a tightening close-up of a woman's body caught in lantana, a notorious feral pest, which is thorny and choking beneath its pretty flowers. For anyone who grew up in Sydney, the title itself plays on sharp sense memories: of the penetrative stink of these plants when bruised, of human intrusion and damp secrecy mixed up in the scraps of garbage and old clothing that were always caught around their roots. The film also shows a Sydney landscape that is not often represented: its subtropical rainforest, forbidding and broody, overhung by damp limey cliffs. This stretch at the back of the northern beaches has always seemed to radiate a voiceless protest against the picnic benches and sports grounds in its clearings – and it was with an eerie sense of recognition that I read Gai-Mariagal author Dennis Foley's description of the camps and spiritually important sites bulldozed to construct the Wakehurst Parkway. Certainly, as a child, you were aware that no one would help you if you come across bad company in these injured sections of bush.

But if any one story has most captured the paranoid sense of there being something 'not quite right' about Sydney's pockets of eucalypts and river, it was the deaths of Bogle and Chandler. On New Year's Eve, 1963, Margaret Chandler and Gilbert Bogle both attended a party in Chatswood. Chandler's husband Geoffrey had headed on to another party in Balmain, and she and Bogle had paired up. Geoffrey dropped back in later, but soon went home, with the apparent understanding that his wife would leave with Bogle. At four the new pair had driven to the nearby Lane Cove River; although the area was unprepossessing, with steep muddy banks and thinly rooted trees, it was known as a lovers' lane. Several hours later boys searching for golf balls in the morning light found their bodies. Both were undressed, although someone had laid Bogle's clothes on top of him; Chandler was covered by sheets of cardboard. Vomit and faeces surrounded both. It appeared they had been poisoned. It is a sign of the parochial sleepiness of Sydney at this time, and a slovenly infrastructure that remains in place to the present, that autopsies could not be carried out for 36 hours because of the public holiday. By then no toxin could be detected.

The deaths galvanised the city and speculation continued for decades about what might have happened in this dank valley with its unsavoury reputation. (Oddly, my flat-dwelling parents had snuck down here in the dead of night years earlier to bury a favourite cat.) Because Geoffrey Chandler and Bogle were both CSIRO scientists, and Bogle was supposedly working on a Cold War project, poisoning by anti-government agents was one popular theory. Impure LSD was another. The imagination of middle-class Sydney was given a work-out by the fact that Geoffrey Chandler was apparently a knowing party to his wife's infidelity. On the same 'understanding' he'd briefly met up, at the other party attended by the bohemian Sydney 'Push' in raffish Balmain, with a woman with whom he himself was having an affair. Then there was the covering of Chandler's body with the kind of sad refuse that accumulates in such lonely places. Was this the work of a complicit third party, a jealous lover, or one of the peeping toms also known to frequent such spots?

It was only in a 2006 documentary that film maker Peter Butt put forward a plausible theory. He discovered that government scientists had been commissioned in the 1940s to investigate foul odours on this stretch of the Lane Cove River. They found that layers of water, refusing to mix, had caused rapid eruptions of hydrogen sulphide, a broad-spectrum poison that bonds with iron in the body's cells to block oxygen exchange. It is most likely that Bogle and Chandler, after making love in a depression on the bank, on an unusually still night, were overcome by these fumes and staggered about helplessly for some time before they died. Police divers at the scene reported a huge disturbance of the black river sediment, which persisted for eleven days. Nevertheless, the fact also remained that some frequenter of the darkness had interfered afterwards with their bodies.

But the story had long since achieved the resonance of myth, to mobilise every vivid supposition in Sydneysiders' minds about the sullied nature of the bush.

Our downhill neighbours were 'not north shore material', according to our older neighbour on the uphill side. They were originally from Lebanon; she was originally from England. Their first crime had been to cut down the miniature she-oak in the front yard, planted by the previous owner, a First World War veteran with lungs permanently scarred by mustard gas. A new veranda and pool quickly replaced the lawn that he had used a hand mower to keep billiard-table flat. A pergola erased the beds of snapdragons and salvias. Most egregiously, they sometimes entertained here, as our neighbour observed through her binoculars, cooking kebabs with an 'awful' odour. The great irony — apart from the fact that they were highly westernised and engaged in the kind of small business that Prime Minister John Howard, the Dulwich Hill petrol station owner's son, would describe as typically Australian — was that they were early adapters of the very things, the minimal garden and outdoor–indoor entertainment area, that would soon come to define the suburban Sydney 'lifestyle'. The street running along the uphill side of my childhood home is now a long sweep of neo-Tuscan villas with thick balustrade-like fences and almost no gardens, squeezed two or three deep to a block.

It was simple racism, of course, as was her habit of running out onto her veranda to exclaim 'Oh my godfather' when the barbecue was sizzling. But our neighbour's comments revealed with unusual frankness the way the city identifies across four major geographic zones. Originally parishes, these four areas are the north shore, the south, and the eastern and western suburbs. The categories are powerful and muscular. Within their broad out-lines are smaller areas of local affiliation. In spite of our neighbour's snobbery, it was clear to me by the time I attended high school that we were firmly on the 'lower' north shore – less leafy, more solidly middle-class than the 'upper'. The demarcation line wavered indecisively around the raggedy new suburbs of Frenchs Forest and St Ives, with their fruit barns and semi-rural showgrounds, but was firmly in place by Turramurra. It was most clearly defined by access to the north shore train line, the great social backbone of the upper north; a place of intrigue and first kisses and being devastatingly dropped. There, I knew, as I caught the same school bus for years along the Eastern Valley Way with the other inmates of the lower villages, was where real life was. There was no one new to be met with on the public bus; year after year, the same boy turned his eyelids inside out and left them that way for the half-hour journey. Year after year, the girl who drew on her thighs in texta spat on her friends from the window to say goodbye. It was like being stuck forever in one's allotted medieval guild.

Somewhere east of the Frenchs Forest drive-in, the northern beaches began. In *Summerland*, novelist Malcolm Knox invokes the sense of driving on family holidays in the seventies into this beach zone – a more exhilarating version of philosopher Walter Benjamin's description of the sensation, when passing in Paris from one area to the next, of stepping over an invisible low step on a flight of stairs. For his narrator's transition is made at speed, by car. 'There was a clean break' from civilisation, his hero tells us, heading onto the Mona Vale Road, 'the pale Brady Bunch limits of St Ives behind, the fire-ravaged ocean of wild bush ahead'. The stages unfold like the opening sequence of a television show:

> up past the cop speed traps to scrubby old St Ives
> Showground, speeding the raceway through Terrey

Hills, down Tumbledown Dick Hill ... up again
to the Baha'i Temple, pink and white and gold in
changing sun, our suburban Taj Mahal ... By the
time we reach Mona Vale and the big left turn past
Nat Young's surf shop – its giant curling dumper
painted onto the exterior wall ... my stomach is a
murder of tiny flapping birds.

This is Benjamin's low step, lit by the hyperreal
colours of epic nature; for in semi-wild Sydney,
such shifts are often giant leaps, not only from one
village to the next, but between microclimates, or
even one geological era and another.

In the seventies an aura of wild melancholy still
clung to the beaches strung out along the fish-
and-chip strip of Barrenjoey Road. As hard as it
may be to believe today, most of Sydney's beach
suburbs offered a tougher, more down-at-heel version of the suburban. They played an equivalent
role to today's low-rent Blue Mountains, their
cheap real estate more attractive to many of their
residents than natural beauty; and there were large
patches of industry around them. They were often
tough communities, places to disappear beneath
the radar. Even the sand hills of Bondi, long since
levelled, were home in the 1920s to associates of

Sydney's razor gangs. The La Perouse Aboriginal reserve, situated deliberately far away from the city, grew into a depression-era shanty-town. Collaroy, when Ruth Park and D'Arcy Niland lived there on the smell of an oily rag, without a telephone, was filled with economic refugees from the city and studded with fishing shacks. Botany is a still a mess of industrial cranes, Maroubra plagued by gangs. But Palm Beach, especially in summer, remained a separate enclave even during my childhood, the stamping-ground of self-made millionaires and the products of the leading north shore private schools. Here they made life-long friendships with the children of Sydney's other traditional area of wealth and privilege, the eastern suburbs.

The west was divided differently, by distance. It fell broadly into the 'inner west' and 'western suburbs'. The further from the city centre, the less cachet. 'Westie' was the pejorative term in the seventies and eighties for anyone from the western suburbs proper, the demarcation line somewhere after Croydon, but before Parramatta. Semi-rural Campbelltown, Emu Plains and Penrith, at the end of the western train lines, were the most stigmatised, as friends of mine at university, who had to spend an hour getting home on the city's worst trains, were painfully aware. During the sixties, as the city's western edge was re-zoned, its farmland had been turned into fantasy parks the rest of the city came to visit: stucco El Caballo Blanco with its Andalusian dancing stallions; Australia's Wonderland; Bullen's Animal World; and the African Lion Safari, in the hills near Warragamba Dam, with its oddly apt slogan, 'It's scary but nobody cares'. It was as if these parks, with their threadbare lions and camels, symbolised the area's almost mythical distance, in public perception, from the city's vital life. The African Lion Safari finally closed in 1991, but some of its water buffalo had already escaped and, now wild, still live in the surrounding bush.

The south, or Sutherland shire, was the quietest of the city's four great 'parishes'. If it was thought about at all, it tended to be vaguely associated with Cronulla's surfie culture. The 1992 TV documentary series 'Sylvania Waters' would reveal that pockets of the south had been stealthily acquiring wealth – their proliferating Gold Coast-style waterfront mansions, like the one owned by the squabbling Donaher family, suddenly worth millions in an inflating market. Although incorporating large areas of landlocked poorer suburbs, the area also came to develop a reputation for the Bible-belt values of an aspirational new middle class. Yet unknown to the rest of the city, it had also been evolving a proudly possessive identity as 'the Shire' – an almost tribal affiliation that would only become suddenly visible on 11 December 2005, during the 'Cronulla Riots'.

A fight between Lebanese-Australian men and a lifeguard a week earlier escalated that Sunday into a violent gathering of 5000 people on the beach, many of them non-Arab Australians summoned by a mobile phone text to 'get down to North Cronulla to support Leb and wog bashing day'. It was news to the rest of Sydney that tensions had been simmering between its rapidly growing 'Arab' suburbs and the more established population around them. The beach had become a frontier zone: here young Arab men tried to embrace a freer beach culture, were often rejected by it, and rejected it in turn, allegedly by 'insulting' skimpily dressed western women. The situation had been complicated by global politics post–September 11, as many people of Arab background had found a religious identity forced upon them, and felt in turn forced to defend it. But the situation could also be read as a return of the repressed specific to Sydney's suburbs: SMS technology was able to instantly conjure up the worst side of its psychological division into 'villages'. At the height of the crisis, residents of Lakemba, like the citizens of a besieged town gathering around its citadel, rushed to 'defend' its mosque. On the other side, it became clear that for some time the non-Arab youth of the Shire had been evolving a fundamentalist culture of 'Aussie' suburban values. 'Protecting' it was a new manifestation of the bullying conformity that is the perennial undertow of our suburbs. The irony at the heart of these riots was that in a city swollen by successive waves of immigration. Generations of immigrants past had run the same gauntlet of isolation and assimilation – even 'Poms' not so long ago had had their British accents beaten out of them, while in the seventies being Italian or Greek, those cultures now so embraced by Sydneysiders, was to be remarkably, and pejoratively, foreign. Most of these 'Aussies' now acting out of a sense of aggrieved entitlement must have been descendants of those English, southern European and Balkan schoolyard victims of the past. No doubt their chant, 'We grew here, you flew here', afforded

Indigenous Australians some wry amusement.

Throughout the crisis, anxious interstate and overseas relatives rang friends who had recently moved to Sydney. But the significant thing about it was how quarantined it remained from the rest of the city, who watched with a sense of geographical remove, almost as if these events were unfolding in another country. The 'riot' has largely disappeared from public consciousness now, although its tensions continue to simmer. The incident was shameful, but nevertheless it somehow felt fundamentally different to the entrenched ugliness at the edges of cities like London or Paris. In those cities there is always the sense that this violence is part of their history, that it has a long tail, that it is *personal*. It may be the very fact that Sydney has always lacked a sense of itself as a cosmopolis – a significant world city with philosophical debts to civilisation – that saves its village skirmishes from entrenching themselves in its imagination of itself. This may mean that history is doomed to repeat itself here. But the city's sheer materiality, its flibbertigibbet shallowness, may also save it. The suburbs' oddly narcotic beauty, along with their unselfconscious capacity to forget, might also allow the city to move on.

Like so many schoolchildren in Sydney, I caught cicadas: Yellow Mondays and Green Grocers with heads of such an intense, soft green they looked velvety. Tiny Black Princes were the most elusive, which may have given rise to the legend that there was a chemist somewhere on the north shore who paid top dollar for them. (No one had ever tracked him down.) After seven years in the ground the nymph instars crawl up the trunks of trees to moult, leaving their hunched shells attached to the bark by the thorny claws on their front feet. It is astonishing that their long wings can unfurl, like veined cellophane, from such entrapment. In the playground their noise from the trees above the metal benches was deafening. It seemed calibrated, as if by some electric charge, to the heat. As the day grew hotter, it thrummed and pulsed in ever-building cycles. The cries of the poor victims, separated from their peers and caught by the birds in mid-air, were very different: a quick Morse burst that ended in a chirp of distress.

The cicadas' nursery-rhyme names seemed to have been given to them by someone whose imagination still cleaved to the shadows of an English village. Yellow Monday had a curious pronunciation: *Yellah Mundee*. It made me self-conscious, as if I was imitating the way my father's family said 'Sundee' and 'Mundee', betraying their origins in rural Windsor and, further back, in Dorset. This seemed to confirm my assumption that the name was yet another import from England, like 'New South Wales', that had been awkwardly tacked onto the landscape.

But it now occurs to me: could Yellow Monday be a corruption of the Aboriginal word, 'Yarramundi'? The name pops up in Watkin Tench's account, which I mentioned in my first chapter, of his fruitless 1791 expedition to try to discover if the Hawkesbury and Nepean were in fact the same river (they are). Tench was part of a major contingent of twenty-one men that included Governor Arthur Phillip, Lieutenant Dawes, surgeon White, and the Eora men Colebe and Bolederee. But the expedition, which set out from the governor's home in Rose Hill, as Dawes drolly recounts, quickly turned into farce. The white men, all encumbered, except Governor Phillip, by ten days' rations, gun, blanket and canteen, soon found the going tough. Colebe and Bolederee, on the other hand, 'walked stoutly, appeared but little fatigued, and maintained their spirits admirably, laughing to excess when any of us either tripped or stumbled, misfortunes which much seldomer fell to their lot than ours'. If anyone complained about their guidance they showered him with a choice range of insulting names. (Their favourite term of abuse, Tench records in a footnote, 'was "goninpatta", which signifies "an eater of human excrement". Our language would admit a very concise and familiar translation.')

After several days of travelling this way along the slippery nettle-strewn banks of the river, they came across two Aboriginal men and a boy in their canoes; their wives and more children were on the other side of the river. In a scene remarkable for its conviviality, the men stretched out around the campfire, and the two parties entertained each other. Gomberee, the first man they had sighted, his distinguished face scarred by smallpox, showed a large spear wound in his side that had healed. Some time later, Colebe asked suddenly for a glass of water, which he presented to the other man with Gomberee. Taking a mouthful of water without swallowing, this man sucked repeatedly at Colebe's chest, until he finally spat out a stone. Colebe told the others that he was a 'caradyee', or 'Doctor of renown', who had just removed two splinters from an old spear. The whole Boorooberongal tribe (a clan of the Dharug), Bolederee added, were especially skilled in these powers. The next day, after a virtuosic display of tree-climbing by Gomberee, cutting footholes with an axe, the men 'bade us adieu, in unabated friendship and good humour'. Today the name of that 'caradyee' is rendered as Yarramundi. But throughout his account, Tench spells it 'Yellomundee'.

If anything captures the unsettled, haunted quality of Sydney suburbia, it is the idea that the mutation of Yarramundi's name might somehow, through some strange historical echo, have found its way through generations of children's mouths into our own. It is not hard to imagine the chain of substitutions. Perhaps the English men named these yellow insects as a joke, playing on the 'yellow' in 'Yellomundee' – a joke with an edge, as the word was detached from the man ('gone beyond the meaning of a name', as Slessor might say) and came only to signify the springy sound of Aboriginal language itself. But it's also possible that there was truly a territorial or spiritual connection between Yarramundi and these cicadas; they are particularly prevalent in the Blue Mountains, where I have seen scores clustered in big years on the screen doors of houses. Both spellings of this Dharug man's name would certainly continue to resonate in western Sydney, adhering to a suburb, a bridge, and a national park (at the very least, the cicadas might have taken their name from an association with the nearby town, Yarramundi). And his presence in the record of colonial Sydney did not end with his meeting with Tench: the British knew him as the 'King of the Richmond tribe'. On 18 December 1814, he came to town to attend Governor Macquarie's annual conference for Aborigines. His daughter, Maria, was to marry the convict John Lock, the first legalised interracial marriage, while his son Colebe was the first Aborigine to receive a land grant in Blacktown. (On Colebe's death, Maria Lock would successfully petition Governor Darling for her brother's land. Although she was buried at St Bartholomew's, Prospect – now a looming landmark over the M4 motorway – as the 'Last of the Aboriginals from Blacktown', dozens of families living in Sydney today can trace their lineage, through her, back to Yarramundi and Gomberee.)

If 'Yellomundee' did become, in turn, 'Yellow Monday', the story is a perfect metaphor for our suburbs' forgetfulness; a forgetting that forgets itself. It suggests that the process of colonisation might be more complex than we think: the English words may not have imposed themselves instantly to wipe out a previous Aboriginal history, but instead this memory may have been preserved, in the Indigenous name, only to be forgotten as it was Anglicised. Or perhaps, even more uncannily – through a felicitous combination of homology and haunted instinct – the English name turned itself into a word that recalled the unsettled past. If my speculative fantasy is right, what can this chain of forgotten associations mean?

One possibility they point to is understanding Sydney's climate beyond our four imported seasons. Frances Bodkin, author of *D'harawal Seasons and Climate Cycles*, is a traditional Dharawal descendant from the Bitter Water clan, whose country is the area between Botany Bay, the Cataract River in the Southern Highlands, and the headwaters of the Georges River. She is the inheritor of a system of understanding of weather events through complex cycles and sequences of interaction that has been passed down, through women, for tens of thousands of years. The Dharawal recognise six seasons in the Sydney region: Ngoonungi, when the red waratah blooms (September and October); warm, wet Parra'dowee, when the two-veined hickory wattle flowers and it is unwise to camp by rivers; hot and dry Buran, the flowering time of the single-vein hickory wattle, when meat spoils quickly; wet, cooling Marrai'gang when the purple lillipilli produces its sour berries; frosty Burrugin, flowering season of the forest red gum when eating shellfish is forbidden; and cold and windy Wiritjiribin (around August), when the gossamer wattle blooms and when it is time to prepare for the ceremonies that will take place within the next moon, to celebrate the new beginning.

Within these seasons certain signs or events allow the Dharawal to predict changes in the weather. When koalas start fighting, for example, heat is coming: 'the bigger the fights, the bigger the noise, the hotter the weather'. When the queen wattle trees produce more copious flowers than usual they brace for massive fires. The longer pattern driving all these cycles is the Mudong or life cycle that runs over eleven or twelve years. And, driving those, is the Garuwanga or Dreaming cycle of about 12 000 to 20 000 years. In 2008 Bodkin became worried by signs she had been noticing over a three-year period. The Aurora Australis appeared over Sydney, followed by the three sisters (planets) dancing in a line. 'The next thing was the massive numbers of cicadas', Bodkin told an interviewer. 'Now those three things coming up together within a year or two of each other were… quite alarming and indicated a very, very bad drought.' Among the cicadas, no doubt, were the Yellow Mondays. It is a strange feeling to think that our playground pronunciation of 'Yellow Monday' might have reverberated with the echoes of this ancient knowledge.

In fact, what makes us uneasy in the bush suburbs may not be so much their emptiness, or wildness, but that they are full of such echoes. One of the interesting things about cicadas is that they sing in chorus in order to hide each individual member within a wall of sound. It is irresistibly tempting to extend this metaphor to account for our almost pathological suburban desire for bland sameness. Perhaps seeing nothing more than ourselves when we look at the bush most unnerves us, far more than its wildness. The more our voices echo back at us, the more we feel the perverse urge to cluster together, to sing the same songs together more loudly, to drown these echoes out.

From the middle of last century Sydney's western suburbs became the repository, in the rest of the city's mind, for all that it repressed; especially, when I was growing up, those on the notorious Blacktown to Mount Druitt train line. Now if the word 'westie' is heard at all, it is more likely to be appropriated proudly from within. For, thanks to rising property prices, these suburbs have become more comfortable, and more embraced as part of the city. Its badlands still exist, but have moved more to the south-west, thanks to the strategy in place since the eighties of building public housing as far as possible from the inner-city, creating pockets of disadvantage far from public transport, opportunity, and the public eye. Sydney's size, and obsession with its gentrifying inner zone, have also meant that it has long managed to put out of mind, unless there is a crisis, the fact that its further reaches are still dangerous places, for anyone of the wrong gender or ethnicity or age who steps over their invisible boundaries, which are often fiercely controlled by gangs of young men fuelled by a sense of grievance and disadvantage.

On Sunday 2 February 1986, this savage

underside would emerge in a way that traumatised the city. Anita Cobby had an early dinner with work friends near Central station, and left them to catch the train. It was a hot night; the temperature had hit 38.5°C earlier that day. Cobby, who had been living with her parents in Blacktown since her marriage recently ended, would often call her father, Garry Lynch, from the station to come and pick her up from a late train. But he did not hear from her, and assumed she had stayed in town with friends. While it was still dark, he would later recall, he woke briefly and noticed that the clouds had taken the shape of an unspeakably evil face. It unnerved him. The next afternoon, when Sydney Hospital rang to see why Cobby had not turned up for her shift as a microsurgery nurse, Garry Lynch filed a missing persons report.

On the morning of 4 February, in nearby semi-rural Prospect, farmer John Reen noticed that his cattle were standing in a circle around something in the Boiler Paddock. Cows are naturally curious. Assuming they had found a kangaroo, he went about his chores. When he saw they were still milling in the same configuration in the afternoon, he went to take a look. He found Cobby, lying face down, her head on one arm. Her eyes were open. The coroner's report would detail her injuries. There were extensive contusions to her head, breasts, face, shoulders, groin and legs. Her anus was lacerated. Both her eyes, her left thigh and leg, and her left arm were bruised. A 12 cm wound on her back was consistent with contact with a barbed-wire fence. Her left hand carried defensive wounds; two fingers had been opened to the bone, where she had tried to stop the three major lacerations to her throat, the largest 30 cm long. One cut on the right side had completely destroyed all tissues, muscles, nerves, arteries and veins. Yet she was probably still conscious as she bled to death.

Over the next weeks, during the massive manhunt that followed, Cobby's beautiful face, radiating the healthy openness of an era, was all over the papers. It is still impossible to forget seeing these photos – on buses, in kitchens and lounge rooms, in hot trains – as Anita, a young sheen on her collarbones, sat on a boat with her dog in her lap, or stood draped in the old-fashioned sash of Miss Western Suburbs Charity Queen. She could have been one of the slightly older models in *Cleo* magazine that my generation emulated: the shiny foundation and plucked eyebrows; the great mane of hair; the straight-legged jeans and buttoned singlet top that she was last reported wearing. In every picture she was poised, graceful, put together. This was a part of the fundamental, almost mythic, horror, around her death. The city had taken something lovely and destroyed it.

The police finally charged five men. John Travers, Michael Murdoch, and the brothers Michael, Gary and Les Murphy were the embodiment of the city's nightmares – pathologically bonded, random in their impulses, and pitiless. Michael Murphy's childhood offered a virtual map of Sydney's disadvantaged places, which then included much more of the inner city: Little Bay, near La Perouse, where he was briefly farmed out to grandparents; then-working-class Erskineville and Rozelle; and a Housing Commission property in Doonside, where he would meet Murdoch and the ringleader Travers. Travers's childhood in Mt Druitt, the most demonised of all Sydney's western suburbs, was a case study of neglect: a mother too obese to care for herself who sat in the dark; seven children left to bring themselves up; welfare payments supplemented by chickens stolen from neighbours. Travers ruled the neighbourhood with fear, and was proud of his reputation as a rapist of both men and women. Working in the local abattoir, he had begun to bring home stolen lambs and pigs, also abusing them before he cut their throats. His casual brutality was perhaps best summed up by the names of his two pet bull terriers: 'Arse' and 'Cunt'. Travers and Murdoch had formed a 'blood brother' relationship, which they believed strengthened by having sex with the same woman at once.

It is difficult, even decades later, to read about Cobby's last hours. It had been a random impulse that had led the gang, who had planned only to rob her, to pull her into the Kingswood. By the time the men stopped at a garage for petrol on their way to the paddock she was already brutalised and naked. Yet still she might have lived if the teenagers who had heard her screams and driven around looking for the car had been able to find it. Another young man and his girlfriend also later searched for her for hours, heading first to Reen Road, a well-known lovers' lane; tragically they would realise long afterward that they had actually seen the car involved, but had been searching for one of the wrong description. Boiler Paddock, where Anita would suffer such a lonely death, was only three minutes from the busy Great Western Highway, the predecessor of the M4 motorway.

Press photographs of the field, with its dry grass and sparse gums, still have the power to terrify. I was nineteen when Cobby was murdered, and my walk home from King Street, Newtown, to Stanmore took me down a poorly lit street that ran along the edge of the train lines that roared through to the west, above black pedestrian tunnels. Some journalists found it mysterious that Cobby had chosen to walk home that night from the station, but there was no mystery about it: it was a summer night. Most Sydney women knew the feeling of freedom that came from their own company on nights when the air was like silk on the skin, and it was possible to smell cooling bricks and sprinklers hissing on suburban lawns. Yet we also had an image, at the back of our minds, of this dark alternate destination, especially at that time before mobile phones. The end point of Cobby's walk from the brightly lit shopping centre into dark suburban streets could, but for luck, have been our own.

Yet is important not to forget the often underrated suburban virtues that also emerged at this horrible time from the same place that had bred Anita's killers. For Sydney's generosity can be as great as its cruelties. Those young men and women had tried their hardest to find Anita. And the extraordinary courage of Travers's 'aunt' would lead to his arrest. A recovering junkie, when she arranged to meet secretly with a detective at the local RSL, she had been less afraid of the danger to herself than the thought that he would judge her for the track marks on her arms. Although she felt some tenderness and responsibility towards Travers, he had intimidated her for years with his boasts of rape and violence. Nonetheless, she fought down her terror and her affection, to wear a wire into Travers's cell and record the confession that was used at his trial to secure his conviction; and during that trial, in which she testified, she would endure years in witness protection and threats from his friends. In the end, she would have to leave Sydney with her children. Amy and Garry Lynch (who had said to police that he could not wish it had not been Anita who was killed, because then it would be 'someone else's daughter') were to become advocates for victims of violent crime, through the Homicide Victims Support Group. Garry died at the age of ninety, in 2008, after a long battle with dementia. Anita's mother and sister survive her. She would have been fifty-one this year.

How do you find a way of capturing all the things that go on in our suburbs — their passions and pleasures, their terrors and forgetting? It is Patrick White I find myself turning to again; who, in a happy coincidence, set his 'Sarsaparilla' novels, *Voss* and *Riders in the Chariot*, in Branwhite Clarke's old parish of Castle Hill. When they first arrived together in Australia in 1949, White and Lascaris, both thirty-seven, bought an old piggery there, and called it 'Dogwoods'. It was to be their first proper home after eight years together. White was not yet a successful writer. His novels barely sold overseas and were dismissed by critics here. Having decided to give up fiction and concentrate on making a go of the property, White's focus on daily life in Castle Hill was singular and sharp.

Over the next eighteen years, the men bred schnauzers in the old pig pens; farmed chickens; sold butter and cream; and planted the fields with cabbages and flowers, which Lascaris took to the Sydney markets or they sold from a stall at the front gate. On the one hand it was exhilarating. They watched bushfires race towards the farm, but spare it, and slept naked on the hottest nights on the lawn. The unbearable summer afternoons were sometimes relieved by the southerly, which 'came with a roaring like the sea' to relieve the hot westerly, so that the trees almost turned inside out. There was also the attraction, for inveterate gossip White, that the suburb was still a village in which rich and poor were jumbled together, its farms, factories and cottages mixed together with mean shacks inhabited, as White's biographer writes, by 'no-hopers and mad women, the touched and eccentric, drunks and dying'.

On the other hand, the reserved White felt like a 'foreigner' (although it was Greek-Egyptian Lascaris who attracted attention, and who was advised by the investing judge at his citizenship ceremony not to speak anything but English in public). White also chafed under the consumerism of Sydney, in which, he wrote, the 'mind is the least of possessions', as 'the buttocks of cars grow hourly glassier, food means steak and cake, muscles prevail, and the march of material ugliness does not raise a quiver from the average nerves'.

When White eventually began to write again, it was to create an epic novel that encompassed this secret history of our suburbs. At the beginning of *The Tree of Man* (1956) Stan Parker grubs out his bush block, builds a rude cabin, then travels into the nearest town to bring back a wife. Over the course of Stan and Amy's long lives, two children are born, neighbours appear, and the home they have pioneered is lost to cheap housing, swallowed by the greater city; there are bushfires, floods, and travelling salesmen. The great wonder of White's book, apart from finding a narrative generous enough, like Gabriel Garcia Marquez's *A Hundred Years of Solitude*, to hold the whole history of a town, is that it is full of the suburbs' passions and small triumphs. White grasps their quiet poetry, their consolation. After the 'children were fed, and the milk vessels scalded, and the dishes in the rack', he writes, Amy 'came into her own. [Stan] liked to come along the path, and find her by accident at these times, and linger with her or put his arm awkwardly through hers, and stroll beside her, also awkward at first, till warmth and her acceptance made them part of each other.' These details that White channelled – the births of animals, frosts and fires, the soft flashes of lightning on mountain tops – were the very things Sydney was ashamed of, in its rush to make its suburbs modern and like other, more sophisticated places. And in the stifling gentility of Amy and Stan's daughter Thelma, who trains as a secretary and turns her delicate back on her parents, White seemed to catch the suburbs' dull conformity at its birth.

The Tree of Man went even further: the suburbs could offer revelations. Watching a storm from the veranda one night, Stan Parker suddenly finds the darkness 'full of wonder', of some kind of presence. In his confusion he prays to God, but what moves him appears to come more from the mud and the bush than the heavens: 'he began to know every corner of the darkness', White writes, 'as if it were daylight, and he were in love with the heaving world, down to the last blade of grass'. White had experienced a similar moment in 1951. 'Dogwoods' was failing; as the men both neared forty they had little to show for the grinding manual labour they performed, in army surplus and woollen caps knitted by Lascaris. One rainy summer night, as he was carrying slops out to a new litter of puppies, White fell in the mud. About to curse God, he suddenly experienced a moment of ecstasy, and seemed to feel a presence all around him. From this time on, White would join the ranks of Sydney's special brand of mystics, who, even if they attain grace, or higher meaning, find that in this city it comes mixed with grit and tidal sludge.

In his later novels, White would continue to struggle with his personal notion of faith, an idiosyncratic mix of humility through industry that owed a debt to Protestantism and a love of Sydney's physical textures approaching animism. In *Riders in the Chariot* (1961), his most wild and ambitious novel, he plunged on with the idea that this ordinary semi-rural landscape could offer great spiritual satisfactions. Each of its four characters is blessed with the ability to sense a mysterious 'chariot of fire', whose great wheels 'plough the tranquil fields of the white sky'. There is the holy fool, Miss Hare — a child of nature in an ugly hat, and the heiress of a decaying gothic pile — who has almost become one of the wild creatures whose nests and hollows she grubs among; Mrs Godbold, the English washerwoman, living in a shed with her many children; Alf Dubbo, a sick and broken mission Aborigine, with an ecstatic genius for painting. And Jewish refugee Mordechai Himmelfarb, once a student of the Torah's mysteries before losing his faith at Auschwitz, who works among the smells and noise of the bicycle lamp factory. Their stories build into a kind of thrilling fugue, in which White draws out of this ordinary suburb its mad beauties and pain. 'Sometimes', White writes:

> Miss Hare would stump off into the bush in one
> of the terrible jumpers she wore, of brown ravelled
> wool, and an old, stiff shirt, and would walk, and
> finally sit, always listening and expecting until
> receiving. Then her monstrous limbs would sprout
> in tender growth of young shoots, or long loops
> of insinuating vines, and she would glance down
> at her feet, and frequently discover fur lying there
> from the throes of some sacrifice. If tears ever
> fell from her saurian eyes, and ran down over the
> armature of her skin, she was no longer ridiculous.

Pitching his characters' ungainly postures of ecstasy against the bourgeois addiction to the predictable and circumscribed, White is particularly insightful about the suburban tendency to bully. Through characters like Miss Hare's 'help', the grotesque Mrs Jolley, with her love of violet pastilles and a good cry at the movies, he suggests that the crimped-lipped disapproval they turn on his characters – Himmelfarb will be crucified by his fellow factory workers beneath a jacaranda – may be driven by a violent fear of the landscape's hidden depths.

It would be easy to turn up our noses at White's chariot, to see it as an overblown substitute for a more authentic Aboriginal connection with the land. But the astonishing – the great – thing about his vision is its generosity. In a brutally pre-multicultural era, and before Aboriginal people's citizenship was recognised, White goes out of his way to trace the stories, with their long tail of joy and grief, which Himmelfarb and Dubbo bring to Sarsaparilla. And he does not try to tell us which is 'right'. His 'chariot' is a pliable symbol, to which each character can attach their history and beliefs. It is never explained or pinned down; in fact, the antiquity of the word itself even carries the hint of something that might precede the Christian God.

'When we came to live here', White later wrote of Sydney, 'I felt life was, on the surface, so dreary, ugly, monotonous, there must be a poetry hidden in it to give it purpose, so I set out to find that secret cave'. Out of his own prickly struggle with the city, White wrangled the idea that it has deep satisfactions for all comers, if they are prepared to pay close attention to the textures and material wonders of the place itself (even people without faith, like me, which is why I have such an affection him). *Riders in the Chariot* and *The Tree of Man* put into words, for those of us who have always felt it, the suburbs' potential to both crush and exalt.

A couple of years ago, after a great tragedy in my life, I drove over the Bridge to my old house to see my mother. How many times had I made this journey? I followed my old bus route, down into Northbridge, up, then down into Middle Cove, and up again. There, when I arrived, was the low gate, still catching on its hinge. There were my father's sandstone rockeries, and the gums chewed by cockatoos, and the dull hum of traffic from the highway. It was all so contemptibly familiar, even the planes on their trajectory to the airport, high up in the slight haze of the sky. And that was its great comfort.

My mother calls me to come out to the kitchen. The birds are here. She has brought one of our old saucers, a once-fashionable colour, out of the fridge, with its clump of fatty mince. Always my mother, she stands back while I go out on the ramp, and the magpies, with their knock-knees and high chests, move sideways up the railing.

The yard is the same. The cotoneasters are fruiting. The dwarf cherry blossoms are still refusing to thrive on the steep hill. The neighbours' aging spaniel looks up from the pergola next door. My mother hands me small balls of meat, as the kookaburras land now, like feathered reptiles; then two pairs of butcherbirds, one black, one brown. Since her elderly neighbour has been ill, the lorikeets have also begun to come here. My mother gives me a quartered apple. As I hold it, they eat it to a stub with careful slowness. They make a constant commentary, a tender sound like a wet finger on a mirror, or a cloth cleaning glass. After they press the sweetness from the fruit they let the tiny bits of pulp fall. Their eyes are hopeful, and bright.

Sweating

It is a month before Christmas and Porky's strip club, on Darlinghurst Road, is the only shop to have made a festive effort. There are three trees on its awning, decked in tinsel and blue lights. It is one of those Sydney nights in which a mad energy is brewing. All day the air has been thick and the distances purple. It is still thirty degrees as I walk home at midnight. From a tree in the Fitzroy Gardens, above the El Alamein fountain, one of the koels, which migrate to the city each spring from Indonesia, keeps up its melancholy day-and-night cry with an upward inflection, as if working toward a climax that can never be achieved. Even the harbour smells like sex. Anything is possible. Fire. A riot. Orgasm. Apocalypse. It is only after one o'clock that the Southerly Buster comes at last, and it slams into the dark city. Steamy air is replaced by cold. A door bangs shut. The windows shake so viciously that, in spite of the heat trapped inside the flat, I have to almost close them. The branches on the gum outside thrash wildly. The next morning the floor is covered in thin, burned leaves. The sky is grey. It is the end of the jacaranda flowers.

On hot nights like this, when I was a student, the phone would ring after midnight. 'I'm thirsty.' My friend's voice on the other end was childlike and emphatic. We would leave our essays and drive in her old Datsun to Kellett Street – it was always possible to park in the Cross then – and drink jugs of cocktails beneath the slowly turning ceiling fan.

It has always seemed to me that Sydney is most itself in summer, with its days of intense humidity that break into storms and weeks of rain. Fennel grows to human height by railway tracks. The sea is moody. One day, on the drive to swim at Nielsen Park, the eastern suburbs are a vision of perfection, palm trees and neo-Tuscan mansions gleaming, the harbour a chalice of gold light. It is possible to feel a benign happiness at the sight of the huge private schools perched on the cliff's edge, the Bridge a misty dream beyond, the

sea-planes droning as they take off from Rose Bay.
Within the shark-net, the water is a tranquil jade,
sun bouncing back up from the sand. A day later,
and the weather is dirty. Cats' paws pit the surface of the sea, and rolling waves slap at your face.
The air looks swollen, bruisy. The traffic winding
back down the hill, and through the flat bayside
shopping strips, is intolerably slow. You could kill
the Chinese family in their people-mover, hogging
the right lane as they point out yachts beyond the
sea-wall. You feel contempt for the lobster-red
British tourists, shorts plastered against their legs,
as they trudge with their eskies and deck chairs
toward a free concert in the Domain. This inten-
sity, this unevenness of mood, is almost hormonal.
Everything is breeding. Two years ago, at the end
of Greenwich pier, I saw an unbroken ribbon of
tiny prawns, legs madly rippling, stretching further than the eye could see. Grey baby magpies
run calling to their parents across the grass, with
stilt-like legs and inquisitive high chests. There is
a feeling like puberty in the air: musky, eruptive;
silly as a two-bob watch; given to fits of gloom.

In my early twenties I spent a whole summer
in pitilessly bright Chippendale wearing cheap
bottle-green silk trousers, a silk singlet, and sturdy

shoes. The cloth was like wearing nothing but a second layer of warm air. The shoes let me walk everywhere swiftly; they made me feel certain. The terraces I strode past were still unapologetically pre-heritage, wearing the colours their immigrant owners had given them: mandarin, Aegean blue, violet, purple. As it wound up through Newtown, King Street fell into distinct zones: a student area of notoriously poisonous eateries that morphed into a run of Thai restaurants; a gay belt around Kuleto's Cocktail Bar and the Newtown; old Greek women shopping at the hot bread stores around the junction with Enmore Road; and from here, only the Hopetoun Hotel showing signs of life among the tiny Fijian supermarkets and failing hobby shops, some with squalid student flats in their tops. The Bank Hotel by the train station lit its beer garden with forty-four-gallon drums; for years afterwards it was always possible to find someone I knew there, in that dark concrete yard. A host of images crowd in now. Naked boys chasing cockroaches that had flown through the windows of upstairs terrace rooms so hot the only relief came from pressing your limbs against the bare walls. A friend taking his shirt off in the Court House Hotel to show me the tiny blue tattoos on his brown skin. Evenings sitting on front steps in Balmain or Forest Lodge, as the sun pressed down on the west like a crimson comet.

And now, as I sit at my desk, I feel a force I have been resisting sweep into this book like a change in the weather. It is my violent love for my city, a feeling as irrational as its geographic assertions – a love for its mix of tolerance and dirt, its sunshine with an undertow, its pride in its own darkness. And of course it is tied up, as everyone's version of their city must be, with nostalgia for my youth. Yet surely no other city's pleasures are so bound up with revulsion, or their beauty so dependent on the knowledge of corruption. It is no coincidence that the stonemasons in early Pyrmont classified the grades of Sydney's sandstone as 'hellhole', 'purgatory' and 'paradise'.

If I had to choose a single story to sum up my city, it would be this. It takes place during a sultry dusk in December, several years ago. The light on New South Head Road, a brute gold filtered through fumes, was horizontal, but still strong enough to almost knock me down. Sydney is hostile to walkers, and you would be hard-pressed to find a more difficult place to cross, over eight lanes of cars that pass on either side of the Eastern suburbs railway line, and in and out of the Cross City Tunnel. As I waited for the lights to go through their long cycle, I became aware that the traffic was heavier than usual; in fact, it was at a standstill. Through the glare I began to notice a long convoy, stretching up the hill as far as Edgecliff. The cars all had their headlights on. There were red styrofoam menorahs on the top of some, and 'Happy Hanukkah' banners on others. I realised there must be a celebration on the other side of town. As the lights still refused to change, and the cars idled across the intersection, I became aware of two young men now standing beside me. Tall, bleach-blond, lugging an esky, they radiated a lean sense of menace that might not have been out of place at the Cronulla riots. As the traffic boiled, they peered in at the nearest driver. Hatted, bearded, he nervously peered back. Slowly, they read out the banner on his car. Then their faces broke into grins, and they began to chant and pump their fists: 'Ha-nu-kkah! Ha-nu-kkah!' As the traffic started to move again, the drivers honked their horns back. 'Ha-nu-*kkah*!'

Like most of the city's magnanimities, this was a moment that could have easily gone the other way. The story reminds me of another. In the eighties, in Camperdown, there was a famous piece of graffiti on the car park at the corner of Parramatta and Missenden roads. On the blue wall someone had spray-painted *God hates homos*. Beneath it, another hand had added, *but he loves tabouleh.*

It is this irreverence that I missed terribly in Melbourne, when we moved there at the turn of the nineties. It was good to come back to my hometown a decade later, where, as an editor once said to me, 'you can open up your chest and take a deep breath'. When I first agreed to write this book I made myself a promise that I would not play the cities off against each other, because their rivalry is a cliché, and because I wanted to reflect the truth: while Melbourne regards the northern city as a Gomorrah, Sydney rarely thinks of Melbourne. Yet the fact is that I can imagine neither of these moments occurring south of the border, and they seem to invite me to understand better Sydney's quicksilver wit and ease. A sense of confident inclusion radiates from both. Our city is so big, so golden, each infers, that we do not need to overthink things. This is Sydney at its best, as a

joyful melting pot. Yet a veiled aggression under-
pins the boys' enthusiastic cries of 'Ha-nu-kkah'.
Join our light-heartedness, they suggest, or be
too serious at your peril. That is why the second
graffito is brilliant in harnessing the powers of
the city's enforced brittleness for good. It is the
hate-filled spray-painter who is instead revealed as
abnormal; as too *intense*.

Sydney is allergic to earnestness, and this has
many causes. Perhaps because of the higgledy-
piggledy organisation of the early city that made
social divisions hard to enforce, the peanut gallery
has always been installed closer to the centre of
our public life than in any other Australian city.
It is there in the delight the 1803 *Sydney Gazette*
took in relating undignified accidents, and all the
way through to the pre-tabloid days of the *Sydney
Morning Herald*, whose back page used to run an
annual survey on which streets were the most polluted by dog shit (I lived on two of the top three:
Arundel Street, in Forest Lodge and Abercrombie
Street, in Chippendale). Perhaps because the city
started life in the less hide-bound eighteenth century it has had an abiding affection for the car-
nivalesque over the pious. Even today at the Art
Gallery of New South Wales, gabbing crowds

drown out the speakers as the annual Archibald Prize awards are handed out. The piecemeal, busy nature of our spaces also lends itself to loudness; no quiet hush on the footpaths here, like cloudy Brunswick Street, Fitzroy. But live here and you soon learn that showing-off is only allowed if it is tempered by flippancy. You can observe your own beliefs, celebrate your good fortune outrageously, only as long as you do not do it in a way that implies criticism of others. You do it in private, or you do it with exaggerated parody. The distinctions are subtle, but exist.

Geography contributes, and not only because Sydney's balminess allows a kind of theatre to flourish on its streets – though, certainly, the city has always loved its public 'characters', like Jamaican ferryman Billy Blue, who was an inventive abuser of colonial passersby, or the 'peculiar and vivacious' Flying Pieman, William King, who, top hat decorated with streamers, would sell his home-made pastries to passengers boarding the Parramatta steamer at Circular Quay, then sprint 18 miles overland to sell them the remainder as they disembarked.

In Melbourne, that flat, planned city, you can construct a perfectly ordered existence for yourself. There are starched tablecloths in the cafés; transport is predictable; you can even park in town. More than likely, the same pubs you have been visiting for years are relatively untouched by renovation, the same crowd greyer and paunchier beneath their short-sleeved shirts and little hats. The weather may be miserable, but it is more often neutral. It doesn't matter anyway, as many of the city's entertainments — and it still has a vital centre — are reliably indoors. People stay, their friends stay, in the same places. Melburnians structure their lives around the real possibility of satisfaction. In fact, if any new restaurant or pub is mooted, it can cause distress.

It is Sydney's wild mix of the stunning and unplanned, of glitz and rot, by contrast, that gives it its very distinct cultural and intellectual life. In Sydney we are shaped spiritually by damp abrasion and the democracy of grit. The sublime and ridiculous are never far apart. Our pleasures, though at their best beyond compare, are rarely unalloyed with disappointment. There is a high chance at a sunny outdoor café that a bogong moth will dive bomb your perfect cappuccino; or, as happened to me quite recently, it will drown in the cheese on your focaccia, and you will be relieved, at least, as you stop yourself from taking a bite just in time, that the black antennae are not pubic hair. A simple downpour will bring the roads to a standstill, or you will find yourself jammed on the F3 with everyone else heading north for Christmas, even while the dry bush to either side of you thrums with joyful heat, and the bays below turn into tender mirrors. As a result, Sydney may be impatient, pushy, volatile, aggressive – but it is rarely *righteous,* because it is never surprised. We don't engage in the ructions that split the cultural life of other cities; we are too busy, too engaged in getting by. Imperfection and making do are part of our aesthetic. Only Sydney would nickname one of its public artworks, with graphic precision, 'Poo on Sticks' (Ken Unsworth's *Stones Against the Sky,* outside the 'Elan' apartments in Darlinghurst); and only here would a body corporate deal with a heritage order that forbade it from removing the sculpture by repainting it from faecal brown to grey.

The Japanese have coined a word for the fifth taste beyond bitter, sour, salt and sweet: *umami*

('savouriness'). It is brothy, mushroomy, earthy: the smell of cheese, the deepest element of stock. This is the secret force in Sydney's freighted air. It is not just heavy with humidity, but with sulphury mangrove, kelp, the iodine of dead marine animals, humus, salt, and mould. Over the top of this base, made more profound and lingeringly sad by it, are the sweeter smells of eucalyptus and frangipani, jasmine on baking wooden fences, gardenias, and the sun-hot needles of pines. When it has been raining hard it is sometimes possible to smell the layer of fresh water on top of the salt brew of the harbour – although the brackishness is always beneath it, giving a funky body, a pulse almost, to the air.

Of course this is sexual. The whole city is loaded, palpably enlivened by this spunky, ancient and gamey under layer. Its air is both languorous and fervid, for it comes with an almost overwhelming awareness of the city's great forces of life and death. Christina Stead captures this mad tension in her 1944 novel *For Love Alone*, which drew on her Sydney childhood in Watson's Bay, then a tiny fishing village by the South Head. It is high tide as her heroine, Teresa Hawkins, walks the cliffs, filled with the yearning that will eventually drive

her into the arms of the wrong man. The glassy
black sea is too full and swollen to even lap in the
coves; it is filled with 'moonstruck fish, restless,
swarming, so thick in places that the water looked
oily'. As if reflecting this strange ecstasy, courting
couples in the bush around her clinch and writhe.

Sydney's visual artists have also given themselves
over to this moist languor. It may seem surprising
to include Conrad Martens in their number, but
you can almost feel the dense humidity in his
paintings, as it thickens the air over St John's College at Sydney University, or presses down the
bush in Sydney Cove. These oils are as sensual to
me as Brett Whiteley's paintings of hot azure har-
bours, viewed from balconies that seem bent by
sunlight; though these have a special place in my
heart, depicting my childhood view from McMahons Point with paint so thick, so self-involved,
that it seems to capture the polymorphous perver-
sity of childhood itself. This bittersweet depth is
there too, if you look for it, in convict artist Joseph
Lycett's naïve pictures, sometimes criticised for
looking European, which seem instead to me to
accurately capture that moment when the trunks
of the gums catch the last light and seem almost
to become erotically self-aware, beneath their

darkening branches. Looking at them, I can feel the hushing of the bush, in the soft pause before nightfall, when the landscape feels as if it longs to slip free of its skin of heat and light.

Even George Rayner Hoff's ANZAC War Memorial in Hyde Park – the only one in the world in which a soldier is depicted naked – has absorbed this extra flavour, though perversely. In the central bronze sculpture, 'Sacrifice', the soldier swoons back on his plinth, held aloft by three caryatids, offering himself to the earthly pleasures he can no longer have. The sadness of this delicate art deco temple is that he will remain forever young and burnished in his gold-lit chamber, protected from the city's salt and rot.

For, to feel truly alive, Hoff intuits, is to be continually touched by decay. Sydney's hammocky air is the *memento mori* that drives our sex, our partying, our real estate. When it is at its most tender and lovely, its most beautiful, that is precisely when its *umami* touches our every sense – when we worry, wherever we are, that perhaps we should be somewhere else; that we should have more money, more time, more life, more love; be at a better party, have a better view, or be in another city entirely.

'There are spots in Sydney', says one of the gay boys who visit us from Melbourne, 'that feel dirtier than almost anywhere else in the world'. And he is right. In Kings Cross the drunks and junkies lie in caked vomit in the recessed front of the empty bank; and when the plane trees seed in late summer, the fluff adheres to the spatter. The uncovered bins are high with rotting prawn heads and oyster shells. Ibis, their white coats a grubby brown, their stench acrid, root about inside them. The public toilets beneath the police station reek of raw shit, and, if the wind is in the wrong direction, the smell blows, hot and funky, across the park and into the Gazebo Wine Garden. The seeds from the date palms form a thick dust on the footpaths, like Japanese soy bean powder. Pigeons peck in the McDonald's; bats and possums leave feral scent markings on the trees in the park; cigarette butts float in the urine, both animal and human, that pools in the gaps in the footpath bricks around their roots. If it rains, everything washes down the stormwater drains and into the harbour, and it is a good idea not to swim for several days.

Much of the inner city is like this. Perhaps I am particularly aware of it because my aunt kept fifty cats at one time in her home in Drummoyne; as a child there was not an inch of that yard that I could poke a stick into without digging up clots of fur and waste. I have the same sense of dank layers metres deep when I pass many of the terraces and cottages around now-fashionable Surry Hills, Darlinghurst and Newtown. Here, I find myself thinking, as I pass a cramped house with its low gate in Macdonaldtown, is the home of a baby farmer who starved and disposed of the children desperate mothers entrusted to her care. Here, in Rushcutters Bay, I tell myself, with its mock Tudor shingles and separate back door, was the abortionist's house, and here behind it is the courtyard where they bundled the surgery's sad waste. Any history of The Rocks will recount the private wells in people's yards, in which drunks and children sometimes drowned. Look at photographs from the turn-of-the-twentieth-century plague and you will see beside the outhouses the backyard butcheries, chains of sausages hanging in the air, and blood pooling in the gutters. It is all still caught up in the bricks and soil, in so many parts of the city, along with chaff from its granaries, smoke from its factories, and the acrid lining from the brakes of trains.

Of all Australian cities, Sydney has most known poverty and overcrowding. Ruth Park's novel, *The Harp in the South*, which won the *Sydney Morning Herald*'s inaugural novel competition in 1946, told the story of the struggling Darcy family in Surry Hills. Her Irish-Catholic heroes were the respectable poor, yet no one living in such close quarters, in dank homes with peeling cladding, Park pointed out, could avoid the bed bugs that swarmed out of the walls and furniture at night. Park knew what she was writing about. Struggling to survive on writers' earnings during the wartime housing shortage, she and her husband D'Arcy Niland rented a room above an old shop in Devonshire Street, near the corner of Riley, just up from where the Shakespeare Hotel now stands. Park was pregnant, and squeezed into a single bed with Niland; his brother slept in a barber's chair downstairs. The closeness and lack of sun would cause her lifelong kidney problems. Her new daughter failed to thrive until the family moved to the only fresh air they could afford, in remote and phone-less Collaroy.

Sydney knew much of its population lived in

poverty, but it could not bring itself to thank a writer born in New Zealand for pointing out that it had slums. When it was serialised, Park's book was slammed by *Herald* readers as 'immoral' and 'filthy'. It was only later that *The Harp in the South* would go on to become one of the city's most-loved novels. Thanks to Park's writing, these terraces would be knocked down and replaced by the grim Housing Commission units that now stand on Devonshire Street, something Park has admitted to having mixed feelings about.

Sydney likes to deny its history of want, and often forgets that it was a Victorian city with pockets of extreme disadvantage, complete with 'Ragged Schools' that educated working children at night. Only recently, the state government resisted public pressure to retain the name 'The Hungry Mile', for the development of Darling Harbour East, given it by the desperate men who sought work on its docks during the Depression – opting instead for 'Barangaroo' (although the City of Sydney Council, after discussions with the Maritime Union, did redesignate a section of Hickson Road in 2009). Ex-prime minister Paul Keating's urgings to replant the edges of the same development with original native grasses are seen by many as another denial of Sydney's rough port history, as are the repeated calls to get rid of Garden Island's looming black steam crane. This is not just history, of course. Recently, novelist Mandy Sayer wrote in a newspaper column of her meeting with the head of the Plunkett Street Primary School, in Woolloomooloo, where teachers were raising funds to supply fresh fruit to children whose parents could not afford it, only metres from some of the city's most glittering new restaurants and pubs. It can be difficult to distinguish Sydney's vital dirt from neglect; but a good part of the grime, it seems, is not so natural after all.

It is cool inside my friend's lounge room. The art nouveau waratahs on the ceiling have long since turned the yellow of clotted cream, and the paint is peeling from their spiky wreaths of leaves. Owned by an elderly landlady, the house is in the grounds of an old paper factory. Great rolls of it bake on the concrete concourse outside; some are already half-scorched, serially set alight by Leichhardt's hostile youth. There is no side fence. There are no signs of industry from outside the warehouse.

Next to the window, trucks back up to receive dodgy consignments of televisions, pet food and nappies. 'We were like F Scott Fitzgerald's lost generation', my friend says. 'It never occurred to us that free education was a tiny bubble in history. We thought the future was limitless.'

A plane on its descent into Mascot makes the roof tremble for a moment. Like a light, the sun flicks off, then on again. The room smells of mildew, and incense, and disinfectant. A year into the new millennium, my friend is just holding on, in this decaying cottage with its low rent, to the textures of our past.

For it was houses like this that we lived in as students, with their hastily enclosed verandas, plastic bags balled into the gaps of the fibro, and windows too swollen by damp to close. Everything was jerry-built. There were thunderboxes outside, with wooden seats, and bricks that bore a faint hint of the night-soil that was once carried away along the lanes behind them. Indoor toilets had been hastily added in cupboards, beneath stairs, in the crooks of landings. Outdoor paint had been slapped on the skirting boards, but peeled back quickly to reveal thick layers of black mould. There was always a Hills hoist, or tree stump, or some other immovable object out the back that rendered the tiny space unusable; often an old bed frame or rotting bench.

I shared three houses platonically with this friend. There was a one-storey terrace in Stanmore, with Greek tiles over its central archway. The girl whose room I had taken still boarded her pet rats in the walk-in pantry and returned to bathe them in the bathroom sink. She was the first person I met who ironed her clothes with spray deodorant instead of washing them; sometimes she would appear at the door, hold a finger up for silence, and march to the piano to play the tune she had been composing en route. Another was a house-mind while the owner was in rehab, his hundreds of copies of *Pilgrim's Progress* lining the hall, smelling sweetly of mouldy bindings. The house's alcoholic atmosphere soon began to affect us. For the two months we lived here my friend, who scrubbed dishes part-time in the university's staff club, did not wash his clothes, soaked with bleach and scraps of food: even from outside the front door, the smell was overwhelming. When I came home and found the Weetbix box open again on the lounge room floor, where the slugs that came under the door from the dank and ferny garden had found it, I pulled a kitchen knife from the drawer and waved it; horrified, he ran out the front door while I dashed out the back. My favourite was the last house, in Chippendale, which we shared with my partner; it had a purple feature wall and yard filled with huge fennel plants that had reseeded themselves from the wasteland that surrounded tiny Macdonaldtown station behind us. The old walnut bed head that covered the unusable fireplace had a natural pattern in its grain so horrifying that we referred to it as the Cosmic Pig, and eventually turned it around. It still gave us the creeps; perhaps because of the witch who had lived and cast her spells in the front room. It was here I began to write; each day I would buy my lunch for two dollars from the Thai couple who had taken over the Greek sisters' corner shop.

These suburbs were still semi-industrial, with their railway workshops and silos, the houses yet to be hollowed out and renovated. On a single blisteringly hot afternoon, on the long walk back from the discount supermarket by Newtown station, I saw an old man roll up the leg of his blue shorts and urinate against a traffic pole; a large box of fish come off a truck and mash into a paste in the middle of the road; and a dog back up to squeeze a turd onto the low front step of the kebab shop that was the popular late-night snack stop for drunks. Not far away a poet friend lived in a flat of spectacular grubbiness, on the top floor of an old federation mansion, squeezed between the deaf hospital and a detox centre. As he prepared dinner, he would brush, as a reflex, with his left hand at the tiny cockroaches that swarmed up the sides of the chopping block. In his bathroom there was an old gas water-heater that you had to light to take a shower, a toilet squeezed at a precarious angle into the corner, and a lugubrious axolotl that observed from its filthy tank on the washing machine as you performed your ablutions. Late one night, the poet said, he had looked out the window into the moonlit backyard of the deaf hospital, to see a naked game of touch football being played in perfect silence.

The thing is, we loved it. Perhaps my generation was strange, I think now, in making a fetish of filth. What is this, the joke used to run, as one put a hand in one's mouth, fingers waving outward in the air? Answer: breakfast at one of Glebe's then-notorious cafés. (Another friend swore that it always smelled of semen; it is still there.) What is the seediest thing you have ever seen in Sydney? I ask friends my age, and they answer with glee. The Golden Grogan, says one: a competition held by the university's engineering students to defecate in the most creative spot on campus; one year the winner targeted the dryers in a college laundry. Several volunteer 'Trough man', who lay in the urinals at the Mardi Gras party each year: a sight seared on the minds of straight boys of my generation. Perhaps ours was a reverse snobbery, a means of rejecting whitebread Sydney childhoods. Though perhaps it was another way in which Sydney taught us to undercut our pleasures. It was a means of not mooning and thrilling over the deep shade of the gums in the cemetery of the old Newtown church; at the yellow flowers on the paperbarks; at the soft industrial dusks over the water at Glebe Point – all of which we had, quite miraculously, to ourselves.

It would be easy to assume that Sydney's easy-going climate is responsible for attracting its huge gay population. The Beauchamp Hotel on Oxford Street is named, after all, for that enthusiastic cruiser, the seventh Lord Beauchamp: an English bachelor interested in artistic matters, who governed New South Wales from 1899 to 1900. 'The men are splendid athletes', Beauchamp reported:

> like Greek statues. Their skins are tanned by sun
> and wind, and I doubt whether anywhere in the
> world are finer specimens of manhood than in
> Sydney. The lifesavers at the bathing beaches are
> wonderful.

Although marrying on his return to England, Beauchamp would later resign from the House of Lords and flee the country when threatened with a divorce that would make public his privately well-known interest in men. He would become, incidentally, the real inspiration for Lord Marchmain, the disgraced patriarch who lives with his Italian mistress in Venice, in Evelyn Waugh's *Brideshead Revisited*.

The city was certainly a smorgasbord of beats. The Botanic Gardens area was always popular. And from the nineteenth century until after the Second World War the section of Hyde Park between the Archibald Fountain and College Street was a well-known destination; so much so, according to activist Lex Watson, that the footpath was narrowed in 1956 to 'eliminate' gay men. Such possibilities weighed on the city fathers' minds. For many years it was common practice for under-cover police to entrap men in public toilets into reciprocating their advances, often then directing them to a friendly solicitor who would give the officer a kick-back. Oddly, the city's department stores were viewed as equivalent spaces for women. According to *Rugged Angel*, the biography of the state's first policewoman Lillian Armfield, preda-tory older lesbians would find jobs among the inexperienced shopgirls in David Jones in order to recruit.

But like so many aspects of the city's life, Syd-ney's gay history has to be understood in relation to its dark opposite: repression. The beats existed for a reason. Extreme vigilance for any gay activity – the police archives are filled with photographs of cycad-shaded toilet blocks and shadowy tun-nels that invite the imagination to dwell and lurk – carried on from the colony's paranoid fear of the potential convict vice. Sodomy and murder were both punishable by execution: 'For either of these crimes', Governor Arthur Phillip said, 'I would wish to confine the criminal till an opportunity offered of delivering him to the natives of New Zealand, and let them eat him'. Alexander Brown was the first person to be hanged for sodomy, in 1828. As late as 1951, the NSW *Crimes Act* was amended to make 'buggery' a crime (carrying a sentence of fifteen years imprisonment), with or *without* consent, effectively diminishing any legal defence that consent had not been given. The state only decriminalised homosexuality in 1984.

In fact, the Gay and Lesbian Mardi Gras, the city's biggest party outside of New Year's Eve and, more recently, Chinese New Year, might not have come into existence except for a police crackdown, on 24 June 1978, on a march by gay rights protestors — ironically, to commemorate New York's Stonewall riots against police harassment in Greenwich Village. The day had begun with a march by 400 gays and lesbians through the CBD demanding a repeal of anti-gay laws. A public meeting followed. Later that night 2000 men and women chanting, 'Out of the bars, into the streets, join us,' made their way down Oxford Street towards the city. Though they had permission, by the time the march reached Whitlam Square, the police swooped, confiscating the PA system and lead truck. But on this occasion, the community fought back, streaming up College Street to Kings Cross, and gathering more supporters. In

Darlinghurst Road, garbage bin lids flew; bottles smashed. Police removed their numbered badges and laid into the crowd. 'Let them go!' the protestors chanted, following the paddy wagons. It was terrifying, witnesses reported, but also exhilarating. 'I was wild, ecstatic and screaming up and down the street, "Up the lezzos!"' one woman recalls. 'I did get arrested for saying that.' The newspapers published names and many involved lost jobs and friends. It will surprise few residents of NSW to learn that no charges were laid; a year later the police claimed to have lost all paperwork.

Moved to steamy March, Mardi Gras grew into a huge annual event, with marchers spending months on choreography, floats and costumes. And just as reliably each year Uniting Church minister and NSW parliamentarian Fred Nile has led his Festival of Light followers in prayers for rain to fall on the parade. (It is almost always a fine night.) Although he is seen by many as a risible figure these days – and has moved on to trying to halt Muslim immigration – it is worth remembering that Nile came close to getting the event banned in the late eighties, during the height of the AIDS crisis. For in a terrible irony, this disease would decimate the beautiful young men who had come to Sydney to be fabulous – bringing Mardi Gras in the eighties much closer to its religious significance as a brief bacchanal before the sorrows of Ash Wednesday. Sydney, where the losses were largest, was also a community in mourning: before the advent of better science and strong antivirals, the marchers were literally dancing and twirling in the face of death. Yet these were also the great years of Mardi Gras, as it not only cocked a snook at those who wanted to define the group by their disease, but gloriously asserted life. In fact, its after-party would become so popular with young straights that the organising committee would find itself embroiled in fiery debates about whether ticket sales should be limited to gay-only membership lists.

Now Mardi Gras is so firmly on the tourist calendar that members of the police force march, and families bring children to pose with the drag queens in the marshalling area in Hyde Park. Ironically, this mainstreaming has seen the decline of the legendary Oxford Street gay bars like the Albury and Unicorn, now replaced by mixed bars like the Colombian, although rates of violence towards gays and lesbians in the area remain high. Criticised for becoming too 'corporate' and 'money-grabbing', Mardi Gras went back to a more scaled-down, grassroots approach in 2003. Still, its contrary wit distinguishes it from other Mardi Gras parades around the world. Marchers have carried a giant joint, Nicole Kidman's fake nose from *The Hours*, and Vicky Virus, courtesy of the AIDS Council, a skull painted in fantastic fluoro colours in the spirit of the Mexican day of the dead. Politics is a popular subject, with ex-Prime Minister John Howard being memorably depicted on one float as a dog sniffing ex-US President George Bush's bottom. But the most popular float in the history of Mardi Gras was probably the work of the bearded and cross-dressed Sisters of Perpetual Indulgence who, in 1989, as the crowds whistled and roared, marched carrying a six-foot high model of Fred Nile's head, complete with his characteristically vigorous dark hair and eyebrows, on a platter of papier-mâché fruit. It was the 3D equivalent of the anonymous graffitist's 'but he loves tabouleh'.

In 1993, under the title 'Axis of Sequins', the *Sydney Morning Herald* reported on the progress of a float featuring 'Madam Sadam and her weapons of mass seduction'. Conceived in a coffee shop in the seemingly unlikely suburb of Mount Druitt by teacher Kooryn Sheaves, it was constructed in rural Kurrajong Heights by volunteers. Builder Lionel Buckett persuaded a local truck-driver to lend his six-foot rig to be turned into a lime-green tank with golden wheels; the owner then volunteered to drive it in the parade. As a Portuguese singer performed in the turret, sixteen 'Western Sydney Teen Queens' followed, most of them women wearing big black moustaches and 'mullets to add a subtle westie flavour'. The last marcher recruited was a worker from the pound who came to collect a cat from the drain of the community centre where 'sexy Sadam's gay army' was rehearsing, though he opted for the relatively straight role of a masked Prime Minister John Howard. Another of the fifty volunteers was a strict Muslim, who saw the joke but decided not to dance. Decades of wit may have been more effective than protest in winning hearts, and taking the message out into the suburbs. For the record, Buckett, from Bilpin, is straight. 'The rednecks get on with the gays very well', he said. 'It's not a big deal.'

The greatest and most fundamental difference that distinguishes Sydney and its pleasures from other Australian cities is that this is the only one to have known itself as part of the eighteenth century. You can still trace the Georgians' influence on our habits of body and mind. But historian Grace Karskens points out, that era arrived here fraught with internal conflict. The great majority of convicts were from working-class and rural populations, and brought with them a culture that was pre-industrial, and which collided with the values of a more educated officer class. This clash of what French philosopher Foucault called *epistemes*, periods that determine the very condition of possibility of self, is the greatest legacy of Sydney's beginnings – far more than the 'vivid, trashy Grand Guignol' of the penal system, as Robert Hughes calls it.

With its slippery goat tracks and heavily timbered slopes, The Rocks swiftly became home to a convict population that mistrusted government, and had ways of dealing with the problems of daily life that predated Sydney's civil institutions. If a robbery or murder occurred, the residents would band together to try to solve the crime themselves. Home remedies were trusted over the new hospital at the bottom of the cliff, which they referred to as a 'slaughterhouse'. They built their houses to suit themselves, without surveyors. Following rural rather than military time schemes, they organised their working hours, often around the daylight, the seasons, and the tides; in fact, when it rained, the population set aside their work for the government and went off to other private jobs. Suicides were buried at crossroads with a stake through the heart, a detail that more than any other suggests a mindset that was still not so far removed from the medieval. The Rocks citizens were also suspicious of any interventions into their private sexual lives by organised religion. Until well into the nineteenth century, among England's rural and working-class populations, Karskens writes, non-traditional marriages were common and accepted, an arrangement that was particularly advantageous for women, who were able to hold onto their legal right to their children, property and name. It is hardly surprising that so many were keen to avoid formalised marriages in the new colony, as they quickly began to own businesses, like hotels and shops.

It is easy to see how the pragmatism and self-reliance of The Rocks residents lingers as a kind of psychic Tank Stream that runs below our city. 'Ya might want to think twice about borrowing the car', I hear the man in the post office queue behind me say, 'I've got a few speeding fines. One's a doozy. I wasn't licensed at the time… yeah, I might have to do something about that one.' There is a sense in which, somewhat like contemporary Romans, we enjoy the city's anarchic tendencies, the creativity of its corruptions, even as we decry greedy developers and our failing public transport.

Yet from the beginning, on the opposing side were the government and church. In 1798 Governor John Hunter (1795–1800) closed down the colony's first theatre, to which audiences had paid their admittance with meat, flour and spirits, because of its 'corrupting influence'. Governor Macquarie (1810–21) set about renaming the streets, christened with names like Windmill Row and Church Hill by their residents, with more seemly names like Gloucester and Cambridge streets. He ordered fingerboards to be put up so that they would 'henceforth … be known and called *only by the new Names* now given them'.

The eighteenth century left another legacy, which was just as strong: an abiding wowserism. For many of the educated settlers, especially the

Anglican clergy, this was the first time they had come across their fellow citizens' pre-industrial traditions, like common marriage. The result was an almost obsessive wringing of hands at Sydney's 'immorality'. Reverend Richard Johnson, holding the first divine service under a tree in 1788, complained that the convicts stayed away while the soldiers beat their drums in church. In 1806 Reverend Samuel Marsden was moved to come up with the notorious 'Female Register', which classified every woman in the colony as either 'married' or 'concubine': denying even sanctified Catholic or Jewish unions, along with the notion that a single woman could possibly be moral, he arrived at the staggering ratio of 395 to 1035. In a sense Fred Nile was following a long tradition of Protestant ministers when he declared, 'If Jesus wept over Jerusalem, he must be heartbroken over Sydney'.

One way the largely Anglican community of free settlers could elevate itself above this taint was to deny others their sinful pleasures. They did so savagely. For all his Cambridge education, wealth, and one of the most beautiful homes in the city, neo-Gothic Vaucluse House on sunlit Parsley Bay, William Charles Wentworth, because his parents were unmarried convicts, was never admitted into the society of colonial 'exclusives'. He had founded a newspaper, published the first book written by a native-born Australian, and discovered a route over the Blue Mountains with Blaxland and Lawson in 1813 – nevertheless, the wealthy grazier John Macarthur forbade his daughter Elizabeth to marry him. Little wonder that Wentworth would go on to found the Emancipist Party, claiming equal rights for the descendants of convicts, and finally settle in England; although his abiding love of his city would see his body returned to its peaceful crypt in Vaucluse.

The safest refuge for those worried about their social status was in habits of sickly gentility that pervaded all classes: wool suits and corsetry; cups of tea; roast and potatoes – solid things, that harked back to English roots and displayed an almost flamboyant disdain, if flamboyance had been acceptable, for the sensual blandishments of summer. Our wowserism has tended to flare precisely when the city is most in flux; for it has always been about denying Sydney's diversity, and its many fecund strata. Thus we went into one of our most Anglicised phases in the 1920s, shaken up by the First World War and the great strike of 1917. By the thirties we had almost managed to convince ourselves we had always been a 'British' city. Then the Second World War brought huge changes, among them the entry of women into the workforce, and wartime bonhomie with American soldiers, white and black — so conservatism flared strongly again in the fifties. Its pall still fell over the city in my childhood. But the city's moral crackdowns have always also been accompanied by a sense of special privilege among the better-off, as long as they kept their indiscretions private. This was clear at my private school on the lower north shore, whose students could be found on their hands and knees among the broken glass on the floor of the Oaks Hotel in Neutral Bay, often with their teachers — to which the school turned a blind eye, as long as pupils displayed good team spirit at Saturday sports, and hats were worn in public.

My mother was unlucky with eras; being beautiful made her the litmus for a Protestant addiction to the plain and uptight that was particularly harsh on women. When her wartime job in the Canberra Treasury (through which she was supporting her journalism studies) was given back to a returning serviceman, she moved alone to a boarding house in Kirribilli to retrain as a secretary. Yet even then, the suspicion of 'concubinage' still clung to single women: you could not sit unaccompanied in a restaurant or hotel lobby, for the waitress, assuming you were soliciting, would refuse to serve you. For the same reason you could not walk on certain streets by yourself, as her six-foot friend continued to do when she was staying in a hostel in Kings Cross, until she was almost dragged into a car. My mother's lodgings were women-only, the corridors smelling of abstemious eggs boiled in kettles and bowels moved by Epsom salts. Still, a whiff of the illicit hung in her family's mind about them. Once there was an argument with her brother-in-law and sister about whether prostitutes were evil. My mother said she would not cut someone dead for this reason alone. No one in the family spoke to her for months.

For these reasons I have always particularly loved the angry elegance of Jessica Anderson's novel *Tirra Lirra by the River*. Its heroine, Nora Porteous, is a dreamer in dull suburban Brisbane, a maker of semi-abstract embroideries of magpies and night skies, which may be meant to recall Margaret Preston's vivid woodcuts. When she marries Colin, a lawyer, and moves to Sydney with him, it seems like an escape: but Colin, and his north-shore family, set out to strip Nora of every shred of spontaneity and fancy. 'If I had to live here I would die,' she says to Colin, when she sees his dull family home with its tristanias, tightly clipped into toffee apple shapes, on the treeless street. 'Die?' he repeats sarcastically, setting the pace. For she too must be cut down, and made to fit: no little remark will remain unexamined. Colin is addicted to stifling regularity: every warm Saturday, the beach; every cool one, the pictures; every Sunday, regardless of the weather, a visit to his mother and brother in the suburbs. But for a time, while housing is short, Nora finds them a cheap flat in Elizabeth Bay, in one of the old mansions above the naval base ('Bomera', lovingly invoked by Anderson, which still stands on Wylde Street). In the divided mansion next door, she meets a seamstress and a gay window dresser, the heart of its gentle and shifting household. Here Nora is able to talk about art, and fashion, and ideas; and, in the glinting harbour light, she begins to free her sensual side.

But the most unforgettable thing about *Tirra Lirra by the River* is its portrait of Sydney's Protestant middle class and the veiled sadism of its strictures.

'A woman's figure has got to be ruined sooner or later…no matter how good', Nora's mother-in-law remarks of her failure to fall pregnant, as if it is the consequence of her wilful frivolity. It is here she will first crumble, Colin tells Nora, as he stares savagely at her firm young jaw; and it is clear that he finds it unforgivable that it has not crumbled already, as a mark of her buckling down to married life. For what Nora's new family cannot bear about her artistic yearnings is the implied judgment of their own lives. Just who does she think she is? For all our reputation for being relaxed and light-hearted, this question still echoes darkly in Sydney's laughter. Nora is eventually bullied into speaking of her desires with brittle flippancy.

What is especially, viscerally, recognisable about Anderson's novel, is the particular hatred the city of my childhood still served up to women who were seen to have any tickets on themselves. They were expected to be dowdy moral police, or endlessly lectured for embracing the frivolities men took for granted. I can still recall walking with my mother in her well-cut slacks suit, down George Street, as two young men behind us spoke loudly the full length of the block about the inappropriateness of women wearing pants.

And now, suddenly, in my mind's eye, I see my mother sitting in a car at Palm Beach. It is the sixties, and she is recovering from the stillbirth of her first children, my twin brothers; as she waits for my father, she holds her dachshund in her lap. An older man stops to offer an opinion; men did this often then. Perhaps it is her beauty, the sunlight, or her lovely dress that so affronts him. 'You shouldn't be pampering a dog like that. You should be looking after a baby,' he snarls, and continues on his way.

'The most Proddy thing about our childhood I can think of', my friend at the paper factory says, 'was being taken into town, to the Summit restaurant in Australia Square, for your birthday'. He tucks his feet up beneath him, in the brown vinyl chair that has survived through all those share houses. 'Love was not about words, but action. The restaurant *did* something purposeful; it revolved.'

For truly you do not fully understand Sydney's indulgences until you see them developing in a perverse two-step with restraint. The ghostly tug-of-war between the sober habits of the wowsers and the feral masses explains why our pleasures are so baroquely realised, so stridently and so avidly pursued. Sydney is the most over-regulated of Australian cities. Move here from interstate and you will suddenly find your car needs a blue slip, a pink slip, a green slip, and annual inspection. Our liquor laws are equally complicated. Coming here from Melbourne, a bar-owning friend was horrified by the difficulties he faced in trying to set up an open-air street venue for the 2000 Olympics. The red tape was endless. More worrying were the intimidating phone calls and veiled threats he received.

Paradoxically, our bureaucracy is the cause of our dedicated drinking culture. Any system of restrictions so complicated and so petty will encourage more and more inventive ways to get around it. Sydney's legendary drinking stories are legion. On VJ day, 15 August 1945, for example, at *Smith's Weekly* where Kenneth Slessor worked, the staff convinced the publican of the closed Assembly Hotel next door to run a hose up from the back yard to their first-floor window. They drank the cellar dry. Perhaps the city's strictures had something to do, too, with its plague of rorts. So numerous were cons and blackmailing schemes at this time, that the paper's Investigations Department would look for suspicious advertisements and a journalist who specialised in playing suckers would out-con the con artists (they would not be aware they had been caught until they opened the paper and found themselves exposed).

Temperance unions had been campaigning for prohibition since the Victorian era. They finally had some success when six o'clock closing was introduced to improve public morals during the First World War – except rather than sending men home sober and early to their families, as they had hoped, the new closing hours were the start of Sydney's culture of binge-drinking. During the notorious 'six o'clock swill', men would crowd the bars to get as big a skinful as they could between the end of work and early closing. The very architecture of pubs changed as they were turned into liquid feed-lots: gone were their billiard saloons and small rooms, replaced by long bars with troughs at their base for men to piss in as they stood, and hosable tiles on the inner and outer walls for vomit. Smaller and more convivial establishments were unable to compete. The effect of these strictures is still felt. Until only a few years ago, visitors to cafés and small bars had to go through the charade of ordering an item of food – or at least pretending to have the intention of eating – in order for the café to justify a licence. At the same time, compared to other states like Victoria, where anyone with a design degree and a couple of thousand dollars could open up a cool small bar, our licences were outrageously expensive. Only the most cashed-up, or mobbed-up, could afford them.

You could argue that wowserism conjured up the state's most colourful identity, Abe Saffron, or 'Mr Sin'. In 1944, Saffron began his career by buying the West End Hotel in Balmain and the Gladstone Hotel in Darlinghurst. There was a rule against owning more than one pub at once, so he had to become inventive with the books, putting one in a brother's name. Yet because the laws against after-hours trading were so patently petty the police turned a blind eye to their transgression – for a kick-back. Kings Cross, the centre of Saffron's enterprises, had been the hub of organised crime since the razor gangs had moved in with sly grog shops around the First World War. By 1947, when Saffron opened the legendary Roosevelt, a Hollywood-style club, with cigarette girls and tuxedoed waiters, a sophisticated parallel economy was flourishing, in which the most influential people in Sydney (that sense of special privilege) could be relied on to put a word in the right ear, while police hived off healthy percentages from its after-hours liquor sales, illegal baccarat games and brothels. The top of this pyramid stretched up to the state Premier, Robert Askin; at the bottom were the bouncers and standover men. As Saffron's son, Alan, writes in his biography of his father, the result was the 'most corrupt state in Australia'. Abe Saffron, like any good businessman, was 'able to capitalise like no other – after all, he was simply providing entertainment to the masses, in defiance of archaic restrictions'.

Monopoly was the key. The more pubs Saffron acquired, the more alcohol he was able to buy legally – then he could redistribute it illegally to his late-night ventures, without relying on third parties. Inevitably, Saffron expanded into prostitution and sex clubs. He was under police surveillance for years, but in what is almost a cliché of organised crime, he would only ever be jailed, for seventeen months in 1987, for tax evasion.

Saffron, larger than life, and partying in a white suit in his Pink Pussycat Club with Hollywood celebrities, loomed in the city's imagination as the untouchable face of a state grown rotten to the core. The extent of this corruption would be finally revealed with the dismissal of Senior Detective Roger Rogerson from the NSW Police Force in 1986: investigators would discover that senior police officers had been so involved in organised crime that they had given rapist and hit-man Neddy Smith a 'green light' for his activities in NSW. Still, wherever there was crime, the public imagined Saffron. He was rumoured to have been involved in the Ghost Train fire at Luna Park in 1979, although his son denies this. For a very long time he was also thought to have been involved in the disappearance of Juanita Nielsen. Nielsen's unknown fate would become the archetypal story of Sydney's greedy dark side, traumatically tied to a moment that can be thought of as a 'return of the repressed', when Sydney's history of radical private interest seemed to grow all the stronger for its infiltration of the complicated machinery designed to crush it.

Juanita Nielsen was an upper north shore girl, who, like so many other women before her, had come to Kings Cross for its bohemian attractions. The flat-fronted two-up, two-down terrace her father bought her is still standing at 202 Victoria

Street, opposite the Soho Hotel and the steep sandstone Butler Stairs, where a plaque recalls her life. On that western side the wealthy families of doctors and merchants had long since moved out of the huge Victorian terraces perched on the sheer cliff over Woolloomooloo; these had been divided into low-rent flats inhabited by pensioners and working people, unmarried couples, and members of the loosely anarchist Sydney Push. But in 1969 this side of the street had been reclassified as part of the Central Business District by the Askin government, and Frank Theeman, the Osti lingerie magnate-turned developer, had quietly been buying up houses. He planned to demolish them and turn them into high-rise apartment towers with overhead walkways, at a profit of millions; the local council was behind him.

In 1973 an alarmed National Trust moved to classify the street and its buildings as the 'Montmartre of Sydney', and Theeman swiftly issued eviction notices to his residents, who numbered around four hundred. A radio documentary captures their voices, with a working-class inflection one rarely hears in the inner-city these days: there were always children running around then, one older woman says, and 'none of this violence business'. 'As a seaman I travelled a lot', a man recalls, 'but I was always coming home to that beaut pad'. Those who stayed formed the Victoria Street action group, while Juanita Nielsen began relentlessly agitating for the poorer residents in her community newspaper, *NOW*.

Things heated up very quickly. Some were offered small payments to leave, and cramped new rooms elsewhere; others found their belongings missing, or water pipes broken. Police from the Consorting Squad made random visits, looking for drugs. Then chief protestor Arthur King was forced into the boot of a car and held for several days on the south coast, freed on the condition that he quit his association with the group. As the street emptied, only a hard core of squatters remained, behind a system of barricades. But they had achieved a significant victory: the Builders Labourers Federation instituted a series of green bans, meaning no union member would work on the site. These lasted for two years, until 1975, when Jack Mundey was dismissed as the leader of the NSW branch by the national leader Norm Gallagher, who would later be convicted of taking developers' bribes.

The battle seemed to be lost, until Nielsen quickly went to the Water Board Union, and convinced them to enact their own green ban. It is worth pausing here for a moment to note that although Sydney has lost much of its heritage, this did not happen without vehement community opposition; it is also worth remarking how many of the people involved in this action were women, from the women of Hunters Hill who brokered the first historic green bans with the BLF to save Kelly's Bush, to Ruth Park who was motivated to write her *Companion Guide to Sydney* by the sound of jackhammers rampant in her beloved old Sydney. Still, it is hard to get a sense of Nielsen, who remains an elusive presence; a stilted voice on the radio speaking of her years spent abroad before returning to the Cross, which she loved because of its thousands of people; photographs of her with fashionably pale lipstick, thick mascara and jetsetter's beehive. There seem to be no tender observations of her on the record. Instead, one has the sense of a lone operator, obscured by her own glamour, or perhaps her middle-class femaleness. One older woman doorstopped by the television cameras clearly disapproved of her interference. In another interview, recorded not long after her disappearance, the real estate agent who sold her her house struggles painfully, as people did then with any name that seemed faintly exotic, with his pronunciation of her name – 'Yoo-nita'.

On 4 July 1975, Nielsen went to the Carousel nightclub (now the Empire Hotel) on the corner of Roslyn Street and Darlinghurst Road, supposedly to discuss an advertisement for the club in *NOW*. She was never seen again. The number of suspects says a lot about Sydney's rich criminal ecosystem at the time. Some thought of Fred Krahe, former NSW police detective and suspected murderer, who led the team Theeman employed to harass residents from their homes. The Carousel was owned by Saffron, so others felt he was somehow involved, especially as he was rumoured to have lent money to Theeman, a regular patron of another of Saffron's clubs, the Venus Room; then again, James Anderson, who managed the Carousel, owed Theeman thousands. In 2008 journalist Peter Rees claimed to have solved the case in his book *Killing Juanita*. According to Carousel receptionist Loretta Crawford, Nielsen had been shot in a basement storeroom of the club by Anderson, employee Edward Trigg, and another man; this was corroborated by Marilyn (now Monet) King, Trigg's transvestite boyfriend at the time, who claimed Trigg had come home covered in blood, with a false receipt for an advertisement in his pocket. But since the book was published, others have come forward, claiming that Juanita had compiled a dossier on organised crime, and this was the real reason for her death. Police are still suspected of a cover-up: they never investigated the Carousel premises after she disappeared.

Nielsen's body was never found. For decades, it was rumoured that it had been buried under the third runway at Sydney Airport, or ground up for pig food; or interred in the foundations of the new 'Lego Buildings' themselves. For they did go up – although, thanks to her years of agitation, at a third of their planned height of forty-five storeys. They are once more the homes of the wealthy. The community centre in Woolloomooloo is named after her, and each year the Green Party conducts the Juanita Nielsen Memorial Lecture on women activists, in her honour.

The other evening, I was having drinks with a friend in Newtown. It was a warm night in the beer garden, and several cockroaches passed one another along the edge of the parterre. I'd forgotten them, she says; though, after fifteen years of living overseas, there is a delight in her squawk of horror. She has not been back since she used to rent the bottom floor of a boarding house in Balmain, in an old triple-fronted terrace; it was ten minutes from my place in Chippendale, on empty roads, in her old car. There was a bay tree and a bee-hive in the old back garden; a platform bed in the dining room spoke of wild times in the sixties; and three old men who shared a floor upstairs. One day, when she went to take one of them his betting slip, she found him dead by the TV. Today, she tells me, she went back to the old house, and crept down the dunny lane to try to peer over the fence, but it was new and too high.

My friend has moved from the house in the paper factory, I tell her. The kitchen sink had backed up; a pigeon died in the roof and dropped maggots in the bathtub; the landlady had been slow to fix a puncture in the water pipes in the dunny, which directed a thin arterial spray onto anyone sitting on the seat. His new wife from Melbourne tried to tidy the place up, then persuaded him to get a mortgage on a tiny flat in Ashfield.

There must be something wrong with us, we say, to miss all this; when I got out at the station,

I admit, and took a walk around the back streets, it made my heart tight with nostalgia to pass the filthy market with its leather jackets and smell of old shoes, the messy paperbarks, and a flying fox, hanging dead from the power line, silver with flies. But it was nights like this one, we agree, when the air almost seemed to decompose around us, that the best things happened; when sweating bodies met, afternoon drinks turned into foodless dinners, or a shared cigarette on a back step became a night of driving across town between parties.

The thing about this city is that you always feel the dark pull of the earth, along with the urge for sea and sun. Perhaps this is the city's most pleasant haunting. For it is likely that those eighteenth-century farmers and mudlarks also brought with them some primitive version of humoral theory, which understood people as vessels for humours – blood, bile and phlegm – that were always seeking their perfect balance; which were attuned, in turn, to the elements. It cannot have been hard, in this new city where birds dropped out of the sky from the heat, to imagine themselves as part of the tide of planets; as earth, fire, air and water. No wonder the Victorians never quite left their mark on Sydney – there is a fiery madness about our

pleasures, which only flare more wildly the more
they are contained. We burned bright in those
dank streets when we were twenty. As I passed the
parties of young people, picnicking in the large
green common around the cemetery, I admit, I felt
a little jealous.

In his stage-show, *My Generation*, photographer
William Yang tells the following story, which captures my city at its best: here are its Georgian wit,
its theatre, its toughness, its *umami*. Peter Tully was
an artist and jewellery designer and the artistic
director of the Sydney Mardi Gras who, between
1982 and 1986, moved it from a political protest
to a cultural event; believing that art should be
part of everyday life, he encrusted his home iron
with jewels, and designed costumes of outrageous
inventiveness each year (now in the Powerhouse
Museum), with great bright extensions and masks
of day-glo plastic and faux fur and holograms. Tully's friend, artist David McDiarmid, had known
he was HIV-positive for some time. The men
decided to move into a warehouse in Chippendale
together, with the unspoken understanding that

Tully would look after McDiarmid if he got sick. But it was Tully, who thought he was negative, who discovered he had full-blown AIDS; it would take his life in 1992 in Paris, when he was forty-five.

Not long before he left, Tully invited his friends around for a party; they arrived to find him dressed in twinset, spectacles, and hat, as his alter ego, geriatric Aunt Ruby. The theme of the event was 'Tragic Tourist'; a hired bus waited outside.

The first stop, Yang recounts, was Macdonald-town station, whose tunnels extended beneath a drab wasteland of weeds and fennel: 'We had to stop Aunt Ruby from wandering off. She played air guitar a little too vigorously and she took her first tumble of the night.' Next stop were the dowdy toilets at Central Station – here some of the men used the urinals while the aging lady blushed – followed by the sewage works at Malabar. At the Bottoms Up Bar at the Rex Hotel, Yang says, Aunt Ruby 'got quite excited by the strippers on the counter. She lost her false teeth.'

There were pies at Harry's Café de Wheels in Woolloomooloo, then the bus made a final pass by the fire station in Kings Cross, where Ruby cheered too hard, and took her last tumble of the evening. In Yang's photograph, Aunt Ruby is on the floor of the bus, legs akimbo; a friend clasps one of her stockinged calves. 'We all knew this was his farewell party to us', Yang relates, 'it was a little bit sad but it made us laugh all the harder'.

Showing off

The glassy interior of Café Sydney is bright and warm, but a breeze has sprung up outside, threatening to dislodge the sails on the galleria. With its blocky neoclassical façade, Customs House was one of the neglected buildings of my childhood, a virtual relic since the 1960s, cut off from the harbour by the Cahill Expressway, and crowded by the AMP building behind it. Six years ago architects gutted the dim partitioned interiors where hundreds of public servants had once protected us from dangerous imports like *Lolita* and contraceptives, and wedged seams of light into its new public library and restaurants. For all its airy solipsism, the Café is well-named: it is from this point that the Eora are thought to have watched the First Fleet sail in; and, directly below us, the Quay was once first stop for hundreds of sailing ships and sailors, among them Joseph Conrad, probably already thinking of the ideas that would drive his novels, like *Nostromo* and *The Secret Agent*. For immigrants seeking entry, at least if they were not white, the building was a forbidding symbol of Sydney. It was from here, once the *Immigration Restriction Act* took hold in 1901, that officers headed to the dockside, to administer its infamous Dictation Test in any language of their choosing.

It is our friends' wedding anniversary, and, among the gathered actors, writers and public relations people, I find myself sitting next to a young TV producer. *Babe*, she calls me, and grabs my arm to reinforce her points. She is back in Sydney after working for years in Los Angeles, and has bought one of the luxury apartments on the old Walsh Bay wharves, where high-profile owners have recently been taking one another to court over endless renovations. 'A book on Sydney!' she enthuses, when I say what I am writing. Each evening she and her partner sit on the old dock with a bottle of wine. '*Babe*, that's what Sydney's all about', she says '– being able to sit with your feet in the water with a nice wine in your hand'.

Is it? I look around, at the remains of my spanner crab risotto on the table, and the almost-empty harbour beneath us, where great container ships once squeezed beneath the Bridge, and Sicilian fishermen from Woolloomooloo trawled in their tiny boats as late as the 1960s, and I am struck by the feeling that my city may have become a cliché; a sparkling ghost of itself – to have moved from gritty melancholy to permanent self-absorption. Perhaps there is no better place to turn over these thoughts than this sandstone paperweight of a building where, for so many years, the city tried to crack down on its own impure nature, to literally contain itself.

I can date the shift to two moments in 1985. That year I saw my first focaccia, in a graffiti-tagged basement café on Liverpool Street in Darlinghurst, taken there by more sophisticated friends. That same year, Geoffrey Edelsten opened his 24-hour City Medical Centre on Broadway, with its velour sofas and 3000-piece chandelier. Both moments were about the movement of capital around the globe, something Polish-born Conrad, here as first mate on the *Torrens* in 1892, would write about in *Heart of Darkness*: even by the early twentieth century, he suggested, no corner of the world, not even the most remote spot on the map of Africa, was free of colonial commerce, and the imagination that drove it. In 1985, after years of quietus, we were suddenly in the money. Treasurer Paul Keating had floated the dollar, and granted licences to sixteen foreign banks. They chose Sydney as their headquarters, which meant we took over from Melbourne as the financial capital. Those who bought property early would watch their equity increase in the late eighties, as home prices rose a thousand dollars a week. But now, as the decaying city woke to the enlivening kiss of investment, Sydneysiders wanted Italian focaccias. They wanted yachts. They wouldn't mind Keating's imported Zegna suits.

After decades of pseudo-English dowdiness, the city longed for glamour. Edelsten had grasped this early. By 1981 the ex-nightclub owner, property investor and doctor had amassed a chain of seventeen medical centres around the city; we did not use the word 'branding' back then, but they were instantly recognisable for their purple carpets, fountain-spray lights, black enamel reception desks and playboy couches. So was Edelsten, in his white suits, with his slightly bouffant silver hair and, by 1985, his beautiful twenty-one-year-old blonde. wife, Leanne. To attend to his empire he used a fleet of limousines, Lamborghinis and a helicopter. That got people talking; being Sydney, the legend quickly established itself that Edelsten's helicopter was pink, which he strenuously denies (it was, he insists, blue and white). Later, he would buy his wife a football team, the Sydney Swans. By the time he opened his landmark seven-storey premises in Broadway, just up from Central, journalists were flocking. The City Medical Centre, they recorded, had a white grand piano in the window (played for fifty hours a week); free jelly beans and coffee; a mammoth TV screen and video machines; a crèche resembling 'a Bedouin tent'; a discotheque; mirrored ceilings; and mink examination couches. All a patient needed was the new green-and-gold Medicare card, for 'bulk billing' had just been introduced.

Edelsten had picked up on an enormous cultural shift: we were no longer afraid of showing off. In fact, our new status as a tourist destination, especially for the Japanese, had ignited our desire to be 'world-class'. Suddenly we were celebrating all things glittery, including our harbour; we were barbequing prawns and a few years later would learn to enjoy our fish without batter at Doyles, in the old Overseas Passenger Terminal at the Quay. Even our Writer's Festival, starting up in the dank bowels of the Town Hall, would publish its speeches as *The View from Tinsel Town*; the cover image was a loose, brightly coloured pencil picture of Sydney in a snow dome, surrounded by scribbled fireworks.

Colour was suddenly everywhere, from the 'heritage' paints applied to the old buildings of The Rocks and North Sydney (oranges, ochres and mustards, which now seem more evocative of the eighties than the colonial past) to Ken Done T-shirts and Jenny Kee sweaters with their explosively bright yachts and Australian wildlife motifs (as if to confirm our new sense of importance, Princess Diana would be photographed in 1982 at an English polo match in Kee's yellow, green, red, white and blue 'Koala' jumper). In Milsons Point, the new Billy Blue School of Design took its name from the colonial Jamaican ferryman, for our past, it seemed, was suddenly exciting; the free magazine it distributed around the city captured the era's confidence with its cutting-edge writing combined with free-hand pencil art. There was a similar feeling about the *Sydney Morning Herald*'s illustrations, mock-baroque silhouettes, which, coupled with its cheeky stories, seemed to owe something to the spirit of the old *Sydney Gazette*. We had a view — we *were* the view. We loved our city. In the late eighties the *Herald* would run a scavenger hunt over months for readers, with complicated clues that were each about different parts of Sydney. The last led to the tooth in the Luna Park face. If you were not living here, as by now Prime Minister Paul Keating would say, you were 'camping out'.

These changes even reached the stolid lower north shore. On Saturdays my friend Vicky would take me into town, to the House of John and Merivale, where the shop assistants were surprisingly patient with fifteen-year-olds trying on its high-cut scarlet swimsuits held together by brass rings. They also sold the disco-style suits and plunging frocks some classmates saw when they went to the Jamieson Street Nightclub and Patches. At another school friend's house in suddenly-affluent Balgowlah Heights — bought by the skin of the family's teeth in those seventies suburban land-grabs — their boat shed grew to house two windsurfers, two sea kayaks and three yachts (two small Lasers for the children to race and the family Heron). 'Gourmet' jellybeans appeared in their cupboards. The mother bought an Audi and had an affair; so did the father, though he found himself so overwhelmed by his wife's new confidence that he enrolled in an assertiveness training course (she promptly enrolled in the advanced one). That they were full-fledged creatures of the bull-market would be made clear in 1990, when my friend appeared at the door of my share-house and fell into my arms: 'It's my father', she sobbed. It slowly became clear that he had not died, as I first thought, but invested in Adelaide Steamship shares. The company had just collapsed.

One thing was clear: the old class distinctions in taste, so savagely parodied by Sumner Locke Elliott and Patrick White, no longer held. Everyone was living high on the hog, or at least – a huge change in the city's character – identifying with those who did. Everybody 'from the managing director to the lowliest shift worker' could feel at home in the opulent surroundings of the City Medical Centre, according to its administrator. This was also the message of the 1992 fly-on-the-wall documentary series 'Sylvania

Waters'. Thanks to the rise in property values, its leathery and bickering Donahers found themselves working-class millionaires, and had acquired a glassy Gold-Coast-style precursor to the now-ubiquitous McMansion, a boat named *Blasé* and racing cars to prove it. (Ironically, the program had been made by an English production company to show the crass awfulness of Sydney, in spite of its sun and new cash, but it probably did as much to lure English immigrants to Australia as 'Neighbours'.) Perhaps only the moneyed inner eastern suburbs remained unswayed. In 1989 I was at dinner at a large Vaucluse mansion with the children of an established Sydney family. 'If I had new money', one of them quipped, capturing their sense of grievance and the era's baroque mood perfectly, 'I would buy a helicopter. A rococo one. It would flap.'

Edelsten would be struck off the medical register for professional misconduct in 1988, and jailed two years later for hiring hit man Christopher Dale Flannery ('Mr Rent-a-Kill') to threaten a former patient. His divorce from Leanne, for whom he once bought a mink-lined De Tomaso Pantera sports car, as well as that football team, would also become official that year; she has gone on to remarry and work as an intensive care nurse. But Edelsten had already changed Sydney. If one thing showed how much, it was the indifference with which we watched his 2009 Melbourne wedding to a décolleté young Texan, an extravaganza for which the couple flew in American sitcom actors from 'Seinfeld' and 'The Nanny' to recreate their first meeting. Journalists here reported the event, but it was a two-week wonder. In a city where parents were hiring stretch Hummers for their children's birthdays and doggy day-care was thriving, the wedding barely rated. Our lives were now as gaudy, as self-indulgent, and as invested in the fast lane as his.

For ten years, while my partner and I lived in Melbourne, we had idealised a Sydney of casual pleasures. But the city we returned to — where friends could trace the movements of baristas from one café to the other; and the sticky old hotels of Balmain were filled with gold pressed-lead tiles, perfumed lilies in glass vases and girls in cocktail frocks — was not the city we had left. Certainly, it was the first time we had ever lived in the eastern suburbs; and many of our friends now had children. But suddenly people were proud of being overscheduled. It took weeks to set up drinks or coffee, let alone a dinner. Unlike the piecemeal get-togethers of the past, these meals were extravagant affairs, where pork belly or milk-fed lamb had been 'sourced' from one of the city's boutique butchers. More often, a catch-up dinner was out at an expensive destination restaurant; one certainly no longer just dropped in.

Something had profoundly shifted. It was a shock, visiting my mother, to see a ten-year-old on his paper round, his mother steering the four-wheel-drive while he pitched the papers from the back seat. It was strange to find the old Sydney Showgrounds, whose hot-dog-eating hordes had besieged Patrick White, turned into private film studios with a 'gold class' public cinema (comfortable seats, wine and unlimited soft drinks); even stranger to turn up naïvely to the weekly farmer's market to find it was more like an outdoor delicatessen, with a few paltry tables selling dear organic meat. There was no reason to think the city's outer suburban reaches were much different. Wanting to revisit the cottage on the main street where my late father had been born, and which I had not seen since my teens, I drove with my partner out to Windsor. I couldn't find it. The street was now a mall, with stalls selling folk art in the middle – was there ever a 'folk', I wondered, that had actually stencilled flowers on planters and watering cans? – and Ye Olde Ice Cream Shoppes. The quiet old town had become self-conscious. The fields of nearby Pitt Town Bottoms, with rows of purple and white cabbages in dark Hawkesbury soil, were transforming into large flat-fronted houses of a strangely English aspect. We crawled back along Windsor Road, through those maddening traffic snags that clog the fringes of big cities, past turns to shopping malls and evangelical churches, before hitting Kellyville's treeless white swathes of 'executive homes'.

But it would be a mistake to think the city was not still haunted, perhaps more than ever. For these were old dreams reviving. Sydney has always swelled and puffed with money. And it has always warmed to rogue operators and entrepreneurs. What had changed was the economy of scale and – perhaps I am too romantic – the spaces for contemplation its old ruins had provided. For, once the novelty of tarting up the city's industrial spaces has passed, all that is left is real estate. It seemed the extravagant ironies of the eighties had hardened into something less playful; although, on reflection, they may have been only stage one of a massive surge, in which the market would unleash our repressed pre-industrial urges for unregulated pleasure. For the dark side of the city's Georgian self-sufficiency had always been an abiding intolerance of the halt and weak. When the boom came we began to root – as we had perhaps always done, secretly – for the overdog. 'Hurry up, or I'll break the other one', a young man in a ute yells to my friend as she hobbles over the pedestrian crossing with her broken ankle.

Sydney's traffic has long been a giveaway of our private aggressions; behind the wheels of our cars Sydneysiders for as far back as I can remember have been brisk, impatient, even cruel. Back in the seventies one of my father's clients, on his way home to far-western-suburbs Emu Plains, had been traumatised one night by a truck that butted his bumper bar for kilometres along the old Great Western Highway; a not unusual occurrence. The road toll of small marsupials through areas of bush, like the stretches of the Ku-ring-gai National Park that wind up from Church Point, was another sign that speed and our own needs took priority over the soft and weak creatures of the wild. Still, there is now a sense that we have graduated from sneaky unmonitored behaviour: it has become our due. Perhaps our drivers think they ought to conduct themselves as the drivers do in brash, successful New York – except in that city, standing at the kerb, it is a shock to see cars stop and wait. Back in Sydney, it was a new and breezy sensation to find that drivers dodged around you, at speed, on pedestrian crossings, using you as a kind of human chicane. The message was clear: losers walk.

But Sydney's addiction to the fast lane has had a strange side-effect. It makes the city more spectral, less like a real city than ever before. It is extraordinary, looking back at the Edelsten era, to see the naïvety with which we embraced this first step in the dismantling of the city's infrastructure – for it is now standard to wait in large medical centres without appointments for doctors we barely know, without the inducements of coffee or on-site discos. It did not take us long to move on from the idea that its luxuries should be available to all, to accepting that we should pay for any extra service. We were soon left with all the Americanness of private franchise, but without that country's compensatory habits of neighbourliness; and, as our numbers swelled, without the rules for sharing public space that develop over time in major cities. In a weird contrast to our behaviour on our roads, which we drive as if we are on urgent business, we have become meanderers of malls and streets. Walk along Pitt Street, in the city, and crowds lurch and wander across its narrow pavements like wildebeest. 'Keep to the left!' an old man screamed at a friend the other day: although she was outraged, I felt privately that he had a point, for I remembered the strict segregation of the footpaths of my childhood, even though they were less crowded then. I am aware of my own hypocrisy: in spite of my lip-service to the city's messiness, this brisk mindfulness in the way we moved through Sydney is one of the things I most miss now. The fast clip along its blocks, beside my father, made it feel purposeful and real.

A trip to the fish markets in Pyrmont confirms my sense that the city has become somehow less substantial. Once a place where one came unthinkingly for cheap fish – even as students we would walk down fumy St Johns Road, past its old wharves and fuel tanks, for a bag of prawns – it is now a kind of seafood theme-park, the deathly twin of the aquarium at Darling Harbour. The oily harbour, the ibis in the bins and the small, oozing parking lot remain; but into this already decrepit space are squeezed seafood cooking schools and pelican feedings, oyster bars and food tours. It requires a visit in the early hours to avoid the tourists gorging themselves on cut-price jumbo platters of lobster mornay. Each Christmas and Easter, television stations dispatch their presenters to speculate on the size of the crowds that will make the ritual pilgrimage, and monitor the traffic jams that choke the overpasses onto the Glebe Island Bridge and beyond. This is a great contrast to the way Melburnians use their dozens of functional and no-nonsense markets, from South Melbourne to Preston and St Andrews. They are still a normal part of life. Stand in the Queen Victoria Market there, looking at the greens from the Mornington Peninsula that almost seem to emit their own chlorophyllic light, or tomatoes with sun still in their skins, and you are struck by how old the food is that we eat in Sydney. It looks as if it has spent days, possibly weeks, in a holding pattern on some ring road.

One reason for our poor food is that that we have sacrificed much of our rich Hawkesbury food bowl, under developers' pressure, to plus-size housing. But the more fundamental difference is that, instead of treating quality as a basic expectation, we have turned poor supply into an opportunity – for those who can – to buy 'gold class'. No other Australian city's populace makes such a production out of being able to run to ground hiramasa king fish, Bangalow pork, or organic spice mix. Driving around town, to 'name' butchers in Mascot or Leichhardt, or the specialty fishmonger in Maroubra, is the mark of a good host. Supermarkets, it seems, are also for losers; or at least for the days of the week when we are not cooking for others or dining out.

We were a busy Victorian city once; but, even then, we did not seem to quite believe it. The Cahill Expressway, which now cuts through the sandstone rise of the Domain, was once Fig Tree Avenue, lined in 1879 by a Turkish Bazaar, Japanese Tea House and Oyster Saloon for the Sydney International Exhibition. Looming above it, facing onto Macquarie Street, was the Garden Palace. Colonial architect James Barnet, who would go on to design Customs House, along with the GPO, had modelled the huge building on London's Crystal Palace. It had the largest dome in the southern hemisphere. Its long galleries displayed Europe's industry and craftwork: glass, textiles, timber and iron. More than a million visitors – half the population of Australia at the time – would attend its daily recitals, visit the Fijian Cannibal Village, and drink at the Austro-Hungarian Wine and Beer Tasting Hall. (Though some of these masses, critics pointed out, had the poor taste to bring their own lunches, and leave the greasy wrappers on the ground.)

Sydney was firmly plugged into the first big global boom: the same boom that would lure my two grandfathers to jump ship here, and almost tempted Conrad, who seriously considered a Sydney businessman's offer to sponsor him trading in Indonesia. The pound sterling, our legal currency at the time, was pouring into the city from British investors. The Garden Palace was a symbol of our success, proof that we were floating on an *acqua alta* of money. The first building to make use of the harbour as its focus, it was soon the city's most recognisable icon, both at home and abroad. What better way to shrug off our cramped Georgian beginnings than to erect a grand Victorian building that would not look out of place in Manchester or Liverpool, as its cheerleaders never tired of pointing out?

If anything captures the freighting of our dreams with thoughts of elsewhere it is this building, with its mad mix of other places. We have long been troubled by the sense that we could be another, better city. Drive along New South Head Road, and it offers a panorama of the phantom places that we have imagined as more exciting than our own: the palms of Vaucluse, which were probably intended less to invoke Hollywood, when they were planted, than the Mediterranean; the mission-style 1920s units of Double Bay and Edgecliff, which had the American jazz age in mind; up through the Cross, where the same wild American optimism of wartime that saw the suburb name its flats and restaurants 'Manhattan' and 'The New Yorker' is preserved in its strip clubs' neon and the huge flashing Coke sign; then down, and up, into the city, where the desire to be English still marks the sandstone façades. Now it is probably the Italianate that holds the greatest allure for us, to judge by the 'Tuscanisation' of everything from Vaucluse piles to McMansions, and even the lions' heads and parterres in the courtyards of our pubs.

'Around me, people sit on Italian designer furniture on an Italian marble terrazzo balcony eating grilled scampi and sipping chilled Greco di Tufo', a food critic enthused just the other week about the Manly Pavilion. 'It's so breathtakingly beautiful I could be in Portofino, Ravello, Amalfi.'

After the Exhibition ended, the Garden Palace was used for balls and storage – but not for long. On 22 September 1882, fourteen-year-old Ethel Pockley looked out her boarding school window for a predicted comet, and saw smoke; then, in minutes, an inferno. 'The lead melted', she wrote to her brother, 'and ran in a stream all along the ground... In about ten minutes the dome fell in with a fearful crash... we could see the flames inside and the statue of the Queen on its foundation stood for such a long time with the flames all around it. It blazed for an hour and a half.' Destroyed with the Department of Railway records and the Linnaean Society's plant collection, were the Reverend Branwhite Clarke's geological field notes, although he did manage to retrieve his scorched fossils from the ruins. As the fire seemed to have been deliberately lit, the usual conspiracy theories piled up: thieves wanted the gold in the geological museum; citizens with convict ancestry had expunged the evidence from the government records; alcohol in preserved fish specimens had ignited; and, most plausibly, wealthy Macquarie Street residents had reclaimed their harbour views.

Yet oddly, for all the praise they had lavished on it, and all its official boosting, the city's residents appeared to delight in the inferno. Charles Harpur wrote a poem about the fire. A booklet of before and after pictures was printed. Artist JC Hoyte painted the watercolour *The Burning of the Garden Palace*. Viewed from a wild promontory on the north shore, the sky is a dusky pink, while the harbour reflects the pale glow of flames that pour from the building's roof. The rest of the city is scarcely visible, as if to make the allegorical point that nature is indifferent to human ambition; that Sydney too could just as easily be taken back. It may be that the ostentatious lack of fit of this imported architecture with the disorderly landscape turned Sydneysiders into precursors of the Reverend Frank Cash, finding it easier to believe in the city's ruin than its glory. Their pleasure in its obliteration may have been an expression of the same impulse that drives the arsonists who set the encircling bush of Sydney alight each year

— an act almost madly parodic of the Indigenous fire practices that once kept it in check — causing thick smoke to crawl up the harbour at night, and burned eucalyptus leaves to rain down on the ocean.

It was in the city's restless nature, perhaps, for its residents to be already thinking of the new buildings that would replace the Garden Palace. But for whatever reason, the building vanished almost instantly from Sydney's memory. The Botanic Gardens were extended to fill its space, with Edwardian picnic shelters and beds of roses. Only its iron gates remain, behind the tiny Pavilion Café on Macquarie Street, marked by a small plaque.

Sydney has never been one place, of course. It has been overflowing with dreams, been different cities to different people, from the start. It has always been a changeful town, haunted by loss, doubled over its own secrets like some strange plasmal marine creature. Even the northern beaches Gai-mariagal clan, according to descendant Dennis Foley, spoke rarely, and with sadness, of the

Gidgingal, people from the east whose dreaming was under the water, swallowed by the prehistoric seas. You could argue that Sydney has always been multicultural, its harbour roughly the dividing point between different language groups. After colonisation, those Eora who survived probably joined allied clans in other country, just as they had during periods of drought; or, like Foley's family, managed to hold onto their own secret, and parallel, economy of stories. The lore he recounts, covering the area from the western edge of Lane Cove River to the northern beaches, was passed on to him in the sixties by his parents and elders, who, after seeking the permission of the 'old people', led him along the still-extant Aboriginal roads that joined the sacred places and boree rings. A decade ago, the fifty-three-year-old recounts, he took his own son to one of these tracks at Oxford Falls, which they found had been destroyed: 'We are a changing people, so we made a new track and maintained our old way', he writes. For Sydney's Aboriginal past is not just about these 'authentic' stories, as moving as they are. The city has played the role of a meeting place for the many Indigenous Australians; the last century at Redfern, but earlier at La Perouse, where other clans joined the original Dharawal, and made a living fishing, and catering to the tourists who came to visit the popular site on a special tram.

For all our official stories of the colony's white beginnings, it was for the first hundred years of its existence a wonderfully varied place, where tattooed Maori oarsmen ferried pilots to meet new boats at the Heads – a truly 'majestic' sight for the 1830s visitor, according to writer Louisa Meredith; and Hawaiian, West Indian and African-American sailors, among many others, roamed the streets. It is a place where, in the colonial era, Muslim worshippers had their own mosque in Phillip Street.

Sometimes these dreams and desires combined in surprising and delightful ways. One of the great citizens of Sydney's Victorian age was the Chinese-Australian tea entrepreneur, Mei Quong Tart. Arriving alone in Melbourne from China as a young boy, Quong Tart had been educated by a Scottish shopkeeper on the Victorian goldfields, and later in his life famously wore a kilt, recited Robbie Burns in his Scots accent at social occasions, and played cricket in full whites. In Sydney, he identified and cornered a market in clean, well-lit and efficient tea rooms, which were particularly popular with women. By 1899 this empire included his flagship Loong Shan Tea House in King Street, the Elite Hall in the Queen Victoria Market (now the Queen Victoria Building), the Gem, and the Central and the Cosy, in, respectively, the Royal and Sydney arcades. He also cleverly decanted tea from the big tea chests, in which it was customarily sold, into small inviting packages emblazoned with his crest of two intertwined hearts. What is fascinating about this extraordinary Victorian – socialite, unofficial ambassador for the Chinese community, and philanthropist – is the way he catered to the city's cosmopolitan dreams of elsewhere, while keeping this vision generous and open.

It is hard to know if Quong Tart's love of all things Scottish was entirely sincere or a canny exercise in branding (the two are not necessarily opposed in Sydney), but it had the effect of both flattering the city's longings for 'Britishness' and playfully transforming them into something exotic. In this respect it almost functioned as another instance of Sydney's long and joyous history of 'drag'. Perhaps it is the case that those who come from elsewhere are able to see the city's ambitions most clearly, and reflect them back to us. No doubt a childhood in New Caledonia allowed Emile Mercier to so clearly skewer Sydney's rickety post-Depression plainness in his cartoons of laundrettes and moth-eaten department stores. Critic Ivor Indyk has suggested that Kenneth Slessor's Jewish ancestry, on his father's side, contributed to his sense of the past in 'Five Bells' as something 'uncertain and unreachable'; but it may also have made the poet particularly acutely attuned, writing about 'gaslight, straw hat, bunch-of-bananas, tram-ride' 1920s Sydney, to the then-aggressively Anglo city's quirks and foibles.

Quong Tart's death would be inglorious, and, coming as it did as the White Australia policy started to take force, seemed to mark the end of a more cosmopolitan phase in the city's life. On the morning of 19 August 1902, he had been working in the offices of the Elite Tea Rooms when a man pretending to be a 'Detective Smith' sprang at him with an iron bar wrapped up in a newspaper and escaped with twenty pounds. Recovering, with his Anglo-Australian wife by his side, in his mansion in Ashfield, Quong Tart was unable to give much of a description of his attacker; but Captain John James, an engineer, who had passed the man on the busy Queen Victoria Market's stairs, was able to make an accurate sketch. Two detectives, who had committed it to memory, apprehended the man on the corner of Park and Castlereagh streets, and he was tried and sent to prison for twelve years. But although Quong Tart returned to public life, he never fully recovered; he died of pleurisy in 1903. Fifteen hundred mourners of different races attended his funeral at Rookwood Cemetery. Two hundred Chinese carried his coffin from his home to a special train waiting at Ashfield station: the Lin Yik Tong hired a band; the Japanese Consul followed the coffin; and several thousand people saluted it as it passed. At Rookwood, forty Freemasons in regalia escorted the coffin, dressed in ferns and greenery by the cemetery manager himself, to the grave, and the Anglican Reverend Soo Hoo Ten read the eulogy in Cantonese. Quong Tart's mansion, 'Gallop House' in Ashfield, is now a home for older Sydneysiders of Chinese descent.

It is almost tempting to see the busy richness of the city today as a 'return' to this earlier, more bustling incarnation. Drive to the Flemington Markets, a kilometre up Parramatta Road from where the M4 to the western suburbs and Blue Mountains begins (significantly, the market is signposted from the west, but not the east), and you will find an entirely different Sydney, crowded with the verve and energy of nineteenth-century Darling Harbour or Surry Hills; one not mesmerised by an increasingly empty harbour view. These unadorned open sheds, with pigeons in the roofs, are one of my favourite places in the city, where Islander families fill their car boots with boxes of root vegetables and fish; Indian women and tough Jamaican teenagers snap the tips off okra, while the girls cheerfully bully the vendors for more plastic bags; short African couples push trolleys; Anglo gay boys buy flowers; and Chinese women, if you hesitate too long over mangoes, will press a ripe one in your hand and walk off laughing. Buying food is not a tourist 'experience' here. And all of these Sydneysiders, many of them new to the city, have brought with them their own stories of love and loss.

Yet before I get carried away, and claim these unglamorous reaches, in which we do not like to see ourselves, as the 'real' Sydney, I realise that a truer vision is probably to be had at the Quay on the weekend, just in front of Customs House. Here, on any Sunday, you will find the footpaths packed with new Indian and Arab citizens, watching the Aboriginal buskers while waiting for the ferry to the zoo, who also seem to be looking searchingly into the harbour for the city's elusive heart.

With forty minutes to go until midnight, on New Year's Eve 2009, I am standing on a crowded rooftop in Potts Point, surrounded by friends, gay men, and Irish and Italian tourists. Embarkation Park, the grassed roof of the Navy car park below us, is filling up with people, and drunken passersby call up for directions. Our host, originally from Venezuela, has made us all bring grapes up from his apartment, twelve each, to be eaten and wished upon at the stroke of midnight. High on the building site next door, two security guards stand and watch the view; a quieter scene than last year when the builders held a party on the unfinished framework, and used the crane to hoist up their slabs of beer. All along the north shore and Mrs Macquarie's Chair, flashbulbs pop and dazzle endlessly. Suddenly, a rogue orange flare goes up, and for a moment the whole harbour hushes, then erupts with catcalls. Someone pulls the cord on a party popper, and streamers fly out over the balustrade.

If there is one symbol of Sydney's apparently unstoppable tendency to adore itself, it is our fireworks. We set them off for everything these days: Chinese New Year, the Writers' Festival and the Festival of Sydney; weddings, parties, Australia Day; Mardi Gras and the finales of television programs. So much for Protestant deferral. In fact, if you want to try to trace the huge changes in the city's emotional flows, fireworks are a good place to start. The city we came back to in 2001 was still feeling the afterglow of the 2000 Olympics. Its overloaded public transport *had* worked, the roads *had* functioned, people *had* been friendly – no matter that this had been brought about by most of the population having to take holidays or work from home for a fortnight; no matter that the blue painted line that marked the course of the marathon had not faded as designed, but still adhered (and adheres) vividly to the roads. After a slump in the nineties, we were back 'on the map'. What was especially surprising was people's slightly dazed air of complacency, as if we had been awarded a gold star for behaviour.

There is something of that feeling in the air now. The display we are waiting for is actually the second, following the 'family' session at nine o'clock. Where once we all gathered at The Rocks, notorious for violence, to see the display set off from Luna Park, now we distribute ourselves more peacefully along the harbour; file agreeably onto the special government buses and trains with our deckchairs; and queue overnight to pass the bag-checks at 'alcohol-free' locations like Mrs Mac-quarie's Chair, which is barricaded for days before the event. Last year, Woollahra Council gated off the long public park in Darling Point, to make it a dry 'family friendly area', and charged steep admission to enter; it was even more of a shock to see tiny, almost secret McKell Park, opposite Clark Island, where locals had been picnicking quietly with wine and rugs for many years, suffer the same fate, though without the admission charge.

These changes reflect fundamental changes in the city's management of the display itself. When I was a child the single barrage was discharged from a pontoon in front of Luna Park, opposite, the blazing cages of light that exploded down over our McMahons Point rooftop — where my par-ents would allow me a dribble of cherry brandy or crème de menthe on ice — like an extension of that lit-up wonderland's unearthly glow. The harbour below turned into an operatic version of Frank Cash's apocalyptic visions, as the sea, the shadows of the pleasure craft cast across it, became a flat mauve-and-green mirror, the flares seeming, uncannily, to bloom up from its depths, as if another, phantom city was being destroyed beneath the surface. Since the nineties the display has become bigger, but less concentrated and more diffuse. Stretching a little further each year, the fireworks are now set off from multiple points along the city's long waterway, on either side of the Harbour Bridge: from Balmain and Darling Harbour; from the rooftops of its office blocks; from Garden Island and Mosman; and the Bridge itself. Once the aim on New Year's Eve was to get as close as possible to the ignition point — but tonight it will be hard to know where to look, as the buildings spout flames, and the explosions break into dancing sequins of light up and down the harbour. The real spectacle these days, it seems, is spectacle itself. The crowd gathers around the water's edge, as much to look at itself, and to feel the world look on.

It would be perverse to yearn for the violent New Year's Eves of the eighties, especially when the night is so pleasantly soft and balmy, and the mood so happy. But I do find myself thinking, as I stand here, that here is another side to Sydney that its messiness has always hidden – it is strangely biddable when it feels loved. To be adored by the world has always been our greatest dream of all. Perhaps the contrarian, ironic place I have always cherished is another phantom; maybe these impulses are not intrinsic to our nature, or the result of lingering existential discomfort. Our aggressions may have come, instead, from a longing for attention; our scruffiness may have been a secret cry to be petted and groomed. Otherwise, why would we tolerate, in this new century, the shutting off of great parts of our city for events like 2007's APEC (Asia-Pacific Economic Co-operation) forum, and 2008's World Youth Day, a week-long internationally franchised religious festival, which saw races at Randwick cancelled by the state government, and 'pilgrims' high on faith singing and marching down our footpaths? For the first time in decades, the Art Gallery of New South Wales was closed on a day other than Christmas or Good Friday, as its façade was turned into 'Jesus before the Sanhedrin', one of thirteen public areas fenced off as Stations of the Cross. Both events had nothing to with the local history of Sydney itself, except that we had been able to attract them.

We must have been lulled by now having some of the highest real-estate prices in the world or why would we stand by as the City of Sydney Council, under its master plan for a 'city of villages', roots out all the secret and delightful corners of our parks to replace them with a neo-corporate land-scaping that dictates footsteps along huge concrete paths where once there was green lawn? In tiny Beare Park, at the foot of Elizabeth Bay, my partner was returning from a paddle in his kayak as the new plans for its refurbishment were unveiled. He arrived, wet and brandishing his paddle, just as the mayor asked for questions. We had dutifully filled in the surveys; we had read the reports. Wasn't it true, my partner asked, that 80 per cent of residents had asked for the park to be left just the way it was? The Mayor's suited assistant consulted his folder: No, it was 85 per cent he cheerfully announced. Two years later, the new park was unveiled, as a band played and tents offered free coffee. New sandstone paths with embedded sculptures and designer up-lights had revamped its deco charm; an interpretive panel showed how pleasant it once was. We had moved out by then, from the apartment that overlooked it. But now the ambos no longer come and drink coffee as they wait in the cul-de-sac for calls; the gay men who used to appear each summer to sunbathe in their thongs on the sea-wall have vanished; and all the new lighting makes it impossible to see the moonlight on the water. Instead, on the weekends, backpackers turn up in big groups with barbeques and stereos. The park, it seems, is now 'world class'. The Council has plans to move on to the Fitzroy Gardens in Kings Cross and relocate the huge, spreading Chinese elm from Maramanah's old garden.

In 1998 a new element was introduced into the midnight fireworks on New Year's Eve: the 'Bridge Event', in which an illuminated image on the Bridge sets the 'theme' for the year. These have included a smiley face, a dove of peace, and a rainbow serpent. But it would be hard to beat the joyful surprise of watching the end of the 1999 fireworks when, just as the bright cascade flaming from the bottom of the roadway seemed exhausted, Arthur Stace's 'Eternity' wrote itself in ascending fiery copperplate across the arch. The gesture was a triumph, honouring one of the city's nocturnal eccentrics. Perfectly moving and perfectly ironic, it literally spanned two centuries, and captured Sydney's warring urges for beauty and destruction. (Its encore, in the service of the 2000 Olympics, at the opening ceremony, was less thrilling.) Yet most Sydneysiders probably do not know that in 2001 the Sydney Council, under its mayor Frank Sartor, copyrighted Stace's symbol under trade-mark law. 'As a public authority, representing the people of Sydney', Sartor said, 'it is important the City takes steps to preserve the integrity of those things that are special to all Sydneysiders'. It is one of the city's great ironies that Stace's rogue marking on the footpath, will only be licensed for 'legitimate' use.

The theme for New Year's Eve 2009 is 'Blue Moon'. I am thinking darkly about these things as the real moon rises to the east through the faint haze of saltpetre still lingering from the nine o'clock session — and it does have the faintest of blue casts. In the last ten minutes the Irish have soaked us with champagne; the Italians have asked my friend Jane out. Someone is calling for a radio, so we can hear the countdown. And then, sud-denly, the 'Bridge Event' jumps into life. On the arch there is the pale blue outline of a circle. As we watch, it begins to quiver and twitch. And for a moment, I put aside my gloom, and am back in the rough city that I love. 'Look at the arsehole!' one of the gay men yells out.

Back in the café, as my friends call for champagne to toast each other, dusk is pinking the sky. In moments, it will turn a deepening royal blue. Below us, the cruise ships at the Quay reverse out of their moorings to begin their slow and dreamlike patrolling of the harbour, where they will cast their reflections on the bays like small, roving Luna Parks. At this time of day all the city's incarnations seem to be present – ancient, sandstone, maritime, gaslight, Deco, metropolis – only to vanish one into the other, before they can be truly known or felt. If I could hold onto every old nail and brick of this place, I think, I would. But this may say more about my own deficiencies than the city. For it is natural for a metropolis to change; as Conrad reminded us in *Heart of Darkness*, the ancient Romans once knew London, the great city of the world when he was writing, as a dark place. My mother, always a great lover of the city's promise, does not have this same urge to hold on tightly to the past, or succumb to cold despair thinking of what is gone. Have I been to Haigh's chocolate shop in the Strand Arcade? she asks me. Have I seen the new Christmas tree in Martin Place?

Yet it seems that the haunted beauty of Sydney does have a peculiar tendency to turn the mind toward the precipice between life and destruction. Branwhite Clarke, coming through the Heads in 1839, already mourned the harbourside trees that would be cut down, and condemned any 'blockhead' who would do so; in the 1930s the Reverend Frank Cash found ecstasy, like the watchers of the Garden Palace fire before him, in the idea of obliteration, while Arthur Stace was driven for forty years to remind us of everlasting hellfire on the footpaths. Slessor missed the madcap Sydney of the twenties; Patrick White feared the mid-century city destroyed the soul. Writing her *Companion Guide to Sydney*, Ruth Park records she was spurred by the

> impulsive urgency about the obsession for demolition, as though no one had thought of any form of change except destruction. 'Oh, my poor old girl!' I used to cry, stepping aside to avoid trucks laden with enormous ironbark beams, black with age and pocked with axe marks. Or I stood behind the barrier and witnessed a stout-set old building collapse in a fury of dust, nothing left standing except the wrought-iron cage of a lift,

and half a marble pediment inscribed with the face of Prince Albert.

Before that, in the sixties, her husband D'Arcy Niland had set out to write his own book, *The Big Smoke*, that would capture a 'true picture of Sydney as she was when I first saw her, a leaky old ship, half-foundering, heading out of the colonial era, and not sure of where she was going'.

Now that populations and money move ever more easily from one place to another, it may be an anachronism to search for a city's character. Yet the sense that global cities induce, that they are Brigadoon-like, a temporary miracle, a mirage, may be, ironically, Sydney's most authentic form of cultural expression. On the one hand, tree poisoners kill the Moreton Bay figs in public parks to preserve their harbour views, while planting 'spite fences' to block others'. On the other, king tides and monster waves eat away at our beaches, and remind us that global warming may make us more like Venice than we could ever have imagined. On the one side are the mourners like myself, who want to hold on to all the things in Sydney that are not for sale, and on the other, the boosters, who celebrate its 'progress'. Yet, in this dialectical city, the two forces sustain each other, and change places. For all my longing for the past, I find Sydney's new heart in low-rise Chinatown with its Friday night markets, and delight in the story that the city's flying foxes, which once navigated by natural landscape features like rivers, now set their course from camps to feeding grounds by highways. I am always happy when I see the illicit human inhabitations that appear around my neighbourhood, like the little open-air room, with chairs and table, someone has built beneath the banana palms on the retaining wall above Elizabeth Bay Road. I am beside myself with delight when I hear that a man has been spotted pleasuring himself in front of Grace Cossington Smith's sober painting *The Sock Knitter* in the Art Gallery of New South Wales, a testament to an erotic imagination in this city that supersedes all bounds.

All these things remind me, as I sit at this table, that this to-and-fro between the permanent and impermanent is what drives us. Only haunted cities are worth living in, as the philosopher Michel de Certeau wrote.

Even the great fiery harbour below us is haunted by its own opposite — Lake Burragorang, four times its size, above the Warragamba Dam.

To form this lake the dam's engineers blocked the Coxs River, which runs through the mountains from Lithgow, and the Wollondilly, whose gorges, according to the Gundungurra, were formed by the epic battle between the giant fish Mirragan and the native cat Gurrangatch. When such a large new body of flat water is introduced into a terrestrial area, according to its chief design engineer, Hans Bandler, the microclimate it replaces changes; so does the river water itself, as it stratifies into different depths. But into the exclusion zone around the lake, stringently policed by the Water Board, animals rarely seen in the wider Sydney area have moved, along, of course with feral cats, dogs and goats.

At the bottom of this lake is the old town of Burragorang, with its orchards and guest houses – its trees, removed for safety reasons before the valley was drowned, were used to build the foundations for the naval docks, just on the other side of the Domain, at Garden Island. Also in this valley, according to Bandler, was a well-known rock painting, 'Hands on the Rock', which depicted a left and right hand, fingers pointing upwards, with four white curved bands beneath them, like ribs; they had been 'carefully prepared by incising the surface to the shape leaving a slightly raised margin around each'. These were not removed before the valley filled. Meanwhile, the dam continues to remind us anew, as its levels drop, of the possibility of our own disappearance.

The city is a great, restless catchment. All these stories pour, when the spillway opens, along the Hawkesbury-Nepean River and into the great 'rip of darkness' below us; and they flow back, into the suburbs, along its tidal rivers and canals. Each jug of water on the table before us holds the touch of sandstone and hands.

Acknowledgments

Quotes from 'Five Bells' by Kenneth Slessor are courtesy of HarperCollins Publishers Australia.

A note on Aboriginal names: Because names held layers of meaning for Indigenous people (who often had several), and because the early colonists recording Aboriginal names did not have any standardised scheme for their transcription, spellings vary greatly (Bennelong, for example, had five names: Governor Phillip recorded them as 'Wo-lar-re-barre, Wog-ul-trowe, Ban-nel-lon, Boinba, Bunde-bunda'; while David Collins listed them as 'Ben-nil-long, Wo-lar-ra-bar-ray, Wo-gul-trow-e, Boinba, and Bun-de-bun-da'). For this reason, I identify the source for each spelling I have used, below.

A note on the tribal, clan and language groupings of the Sydney area: Again, our understanding of the language groups and tribes around the Sydney area at the time of colonisation is not straightforward. Since colonists first recorded them, the boundaries have subsequently been redrawn, as further information has come to light. In addition, because there was no written tradition among the Aboriginal inhabitants, spellings differ.

Sydney Harbour was the meeting point between several major language groups: the Dharug, Dharawal, Gundungurra and Kurringgai. These larger groups were divided into smaller bands or clans. The clans of the Dharug were the Cadigal, Wangal, Burramattagal, Wallumattagal, Muru-ora-dial, Kameygal, Birrabirragal (these clans living around both shores of the harbour also appear to have identified as 'Eora'); also the Borogegal-Yuruey, Bediagal, Bidjigal, Toogagal, Cabrogal, Boorooberongal, Cannemegal, Gomerigal-ton-gara, Muringong, Cattai, Kurrajong, Boo-bain-ora and Mulgoa. The clans of the Kurringgai, in the north, were the Terramerragal, Cammeraigal, Carigal, Cannalgal, Gorualgal and Kayimai. Those of the Dharawal were the Gweagal, Norongerragal, Illawarra, Threawal, Tagary, Wandeandegal,

Ory-ang-ora and Goorungurragal. (These names are all taken from the City of Sydney's 'Barani' Indigenous history website: www.cityofsydney. nsw.gov.au/barani/themes/theme1.htm.)

The word 'Eora' appears to have been a word for 'people', which some Dharug used to refer to themselves. There is contention about the usage of this term. Some Aboriginal people from the Sydney region claim their identity and country as 'Eora', others prefer to identify themselves by their clan name.

Foreword

Tim Parks's account of living in Verona is *Italian Neighbours: An Englishman in Verona* (London: Heinemann, 1992). His description of the Italian sailor screaming *'Mammaaaaa! Mammaaaaa!'* appears on pages 292–93.

David Williamson's play *Emerald City* was first performed in 1987; it was turned into a film in 1988.

Ghosting

Peter Solness's photographs can be viewed at: www.solness.com.au. What appear to be penises in Solness's photograph of the 'lizard man' at

Bondi Golf Course are more likely representations of bags Aboriginal men carried around their loins, holding sacred stones or other objects.

The description of Guy Lynch going 'to pieces' after his brother's death is taken from Peter Kirkpatrick's entry on Joe Lynch (Joseph Young Lynch) in *The Australian Dictionary of Biography*: www.adbonline.anu.edu.au/biogs/A150728b.htm.

The names of Colebe, Bennelong, and Bennelong's wives Arabanoo and Gooroobaroobooloo are taken from the *Australian Dictionary of Biography*.

The exact cause of the 1789 epidemic of smallpox among Port Jackson tribes remains a mystery. Some epidemiologists have suggested that the First Fleet brought the disease; others have speculated that it travelled via trade routes from Macassan fisherman in the country's far north. Conspiracy theorists have even surmised that the infection was deliberately introduced as a form of genocide, since the First Fleet surgeons imported bottles of 'variolous' for inoculations. Its impact on the Indigenous population was devastating. Around Sydney Cove the Cadigal were reduced from fifty to three. Captain John Hunter, of HMS *Sirius*, noted that the rock shelters around the harbour were filled with entire families 'lying dead'.

Patyegarang's name, and those of her companions — Wariwear, Balluderry, Boorong and Kurrubin — are taken from Lieutenant William Dawes's notebooks, with his spellings. Dawes's notebooks have been digitally reproduced online in collaboration between the Hans Rausing Endangered Languages Project and the Library Special Collections of the School of Oriental and African Studies (SOAS) in London. They can be found at www.williamdawes.org/index.html. All quotes are from this source.

Maria Nugent discusses Samuel Bennett's *The History of Australian Discovery and Colonisation* (1865) in *Captain Cook Was Here* (Cambridge: Cambridge University Press, 2009, page 45). I have taken the names of the elderly witnesses to his landing from here.

Thomas Watling's description of the Eora observing him paint appears in his *Letters from an Exile at Botany Bay to His Aunt in Dumfries* (1794): the quote here, from his letter of 12 May 1793, is taken from *The Birth of Sydney*, edited by Tim Flannery (Melbourne: Text, 1999, pages 130–31).

Bennelong and Governor Phillip were also observed to address one another as 'Beanga' and 'Dooroow' — 'Father' and 'Son'. In *Writing Never Arrives Naked: Early Aboriginal Cultures of Writing in*

Australia (Canberra: Aboriginal Studies Press, 2006, page 60), author Penny Van Toorn notes: 'In Bennelong's culture... kinship terms such as father, mother, auntie, uncle, son and daughter are used not only to identify people related "by blood", but also to bring them into kinship relationships with clearly defined rules of behaviour toward one another, other family members and associates.' In *Aboriginal History* (Volume 33, 2009: pages 7–30) Keith Vincent Smith offers a very useful account of Bennelong's wider family and kinships, and names a number of other Aboriginal inhabitants of the Sydney area.

Bennelong's letter to Mr Philips, Lord Sydney's steward, is reproduced in Nicholas Jose (ed.) *The Macquarie PEN Anthology of Australian Literature* (Sydney: Allen & Unwin, 2009, page 60). While the letter is addressed to Philips, Bennelong's 'you' is clearly intended to include Lord and Lady Sydney. In *Writing Never Arrives Naked*, Van Toorn sensitively analyses the ways in which Bennelong's letter can be read as an attempt to find a hybrid form of communication between the official letters he had observed Captain Phillip write, as he lived with him, and Indigenous systems of obligation.

Lieutenant-General Watkin Tench's description

of the 1791 expedition along the Hawkesbury River is taken from his *A Complete Account of the Settlement at Port Jackson, in New South Wales, Including an Accurate Description of the Situation of the Colony; and of its Natural Productions; Taken on the Spot*, which was published in 1793, and published online by Project Gutenberg in 2006 (Ebook 3534), www.gutenberg.org/dirs/3/5/3/3534/3534-h/3534-h.htm.

The deeply strange noir film *Night of the Hunter* (1955) starred Robert Mitchum and silent movie icon Lillian Gish. Distributed by United Artists, this was actor Charles Laughton's first and only work as a director. Mitchum plays a preacher obsessed with carnal sin; he marries widows for their money, then murders them. In the scene I refer to, as his latest victim's children flee him by night, they fall asleep on their boat; as it glides along the moonlit river, as if drawn by some supernatural force, the children are observed by the many wild creatures on the river's banks.

Ruth Park's description of the 'sacred snake' disappearing beneath her outdoor toilet and house in Neutral Bay is from her autobiography *Fishing in the Styx* (Melbourne: Viking, 1993, page 176). On this 'golden rock' there were, in addition, 'pictures of whales, hammerhead sharks, wallabies and lizards'. And in 'the concavities under the house, sculpted by wind and rain, were dim paintings of human beings, one the faded figure of a man with no mouth and a hat shaped like an ice-cream cone. Traces of black and yellow ochre were still discernible.'

The guide to Aboriginal rock carvings, which describes the destruction of those in Point Piper, is Peter Stanbury and John Clegg's *A Field Guide to Aboriginal Rock Engravings* (Melbourne: Oxford University Press, 1990). The guide also, whimsically, features poems by David Campbell.

The tiny midden discovered by a historical archaeologist working in Cumberland Street is described by James Woodford in 'What Lies Beneath' (*Griffith Review*, Edition 20: *Cities on the Edge*, www.griffithreview.com/edition-20/51/60.html).

The Tank Stream may operate as a virtual sewer, but it has a powerful hold on the city's imagination. The Historic Houses Trust's twice-yearly tours are so popular that Sydneysiders compete in an online ballot to join them.

Tim Flannery describes the ripple lines in Sydney sandstone in his introduction to *The Birth of Sydney*, on pages 8–9.

Kenneth Slessor described Sydney as a 'kind of dispersed and vaguer Venice' in his essay, 'A Portrait of Sydney', published in the 1950 book of the same name edited by Gwen Morton Spencer and Sydney Ure Smith. It is reproduced by editor Dennis Haskell in *Kenneth Slessor: Poetry, Essays, War Despatches, War Diaries, Journalism, Autobiographical Material and Letters* (Brisbane: University of Queensland Press, 1991, page 74). On the same page, Slessor writes: 'The water is like silk, like pewter, like blood, like a leopard's skin, and occasionally merely like water. Its pigments run into themselves, from amber and aquamarine through cobalt to the deep and tranquil molasses of a summer midnight. Sometimes it dances with flakes of fire, sometimes it is blank and anonymous with fog, sometimes it shouts as joyously as a mirror.'

Ruth Park's description of cockatoos calling out in 'boys' voices' is from her *Companion Guide to Sydney* (Sydney: Collins, 1973).

Frank Fowler's 1859 memoir, *Southern Lights and Shadows*, is extracted in Flannery's *The Birth of Sydney*. His description of the colony's prolific insect life appears on page 294, and his description of being lighted home by the stars, further on in my chapter, on page 295.

All quotes from Ralph Clark's journal and letters are taken from *The Journal and Letters of Lt. Ralph Clark 1787–1792*, prepared from the print edition published by Australian Documents Library in Association with The Library of Australian History, edited by Paul G Fidlon and RJ Ryan, and published online by the University of Sydney Library: www.setis.library.usyd.edu.au/ozlit/pdf/clajour.pdf.

Cedar Boys, 2009, was written and directed by Serhat Caradee; it was produced by the NSW Film and Television Office, Screen Australia and Templar Films and distributed by Mushroom Pictures. *Cedar Boys* was filmed around the western Sydney suburbs of St Marys, Bankstown, Punchbowl and Wentworthville.

The green bans I mention in relation to The Rocks were put in place by the Builders Labourers Federation (BLF) in the 1970s. In support of residents' groups, unionised construction workers refused to work on construction. The first green ban was enacted in 1971 to protect bushland in Hunters Hill. By 1974, when the ban movement collapsed, the green bans had saved over 100 buildings deemed worthy of preservation by the National Trust; they prevented Centennial Park from being turned into a sports stadium, and the Botanic Gardens (near where Lynch's *Satyr* sits) from becoming a car park for the Sydney Opera House.

Slessor would describe the 'vestigial flamboyance' of Kings Cross in his essay, 'My Kings Cross', collected in Dennis Haskell's *Kenneth Slessor*, page 84. He would also playfully write: 'To me, the Chevron Hilton Hotel, with its glittering windows and huge verticals, is as awe-inspiring as Ayers Rock'.

Arthur Malcolm Stace, the 'eternity man', was born in Redfern in 1885 and died in Pyrmont in 1967. His conversion occurred at the Burton Street Tabernacle, which still stands in Burton Street, Darlinghurst. When he died, Stace bequeathed his savings to the Baptist missions and his body to the University of Sydney's medical school. Given the antiquity of many of the preserved body parts studied by my friends there in the 1980s, it is tempting to wonder if they worked on Stace, and if students may even do so today.

In *Darlinghurst Nights*, Slessor's poem 'Choker's Lane' describes this type of back alley as a 'green and watery' nightmare landscape of doors like 'black and shining coffin-lids' behind which girls stand with 'faces white as zinc'. Kenneth Slessor and Virgil Reilly first published *Darlinghurst Nights* in 1933 with Frank C Johnson Publications; Angus and Robertson released the facsimile edition, from which I quote, in 1971. Virgil Reilly, who signed himself simply 'Virgil', was born in 1892, and began to work for *Smith's Weekly* in the 1920s, where he was best known for his lithe, bobbed, and flimsily-dressed 'Virgil Girl'. A tiny man, he liked to refer to himself in his later years as one of Sydney's 'oldest leprechauns'. When a fire destroyed his Potts Point flat in 1968, along with all his belongings, the city opened a 'Virgil fund'. He died in 1974.

Slessor made his claim to have seen someone shooting at plates from the window of his Elizabeth Bay apartment in his essay, 'My Kings Cross'.

The old mansion 'Maramanah', now part of the Fitzroy Gardens in Kings Cross, was immortalised as the home of the Hollander family in Robin Dalton's much-loved memoir *Aunts up the Cross* (Melbourne: Macmillan, 1998; first published in 1965 under the name Robin Eakin). Dalton's father was the Kings Cross 'gun doc', sometimes called on by the underworld in the middle of the night to patch up its members (their home was further along Darlinghurst Road, and demolished to build Kings Cross Station). The park's earlier incarnation was as part of the Macleay estate (Elizabeth Bay House). 'Maramanah' was sold by the family in 1943 and demolished in 1954.

Eleanor Dark's *Waterway* was first published in 1938. Quote from the 1979 Angus and Robertson edition, page 11.

The poem 'Sung on Seeing Pelicans' is taken from Dawes's notebook, Book C, page 15.

Dreaming

Ralph Clark's reference to the sick convicts is made on 'Munday 28' January 1788. These private diaries, which appear to be addressed to Betsey Alicia with the intention that she would one day read them, depend in part for their touching immediacy on Clark's idiosyncratic and rushed spelling, which I have preserved, as recorded in the online version. Clark was not unusual in seeing the convict women as repugnant and debauched – an attitude Grace Karskens challenges, in her work on The Rocks, cited in my chapter 'Sweating'. Clark dreamed of Betsey Alicia in her 'old Black Silk gown' on Sunday 23 September 1787; of the new drum on Saturday 27 October; and of Betsey walking in a 'Strange Place' on Saturday 29 December. He read of Lady Jane Gray and compared her longingly to Alicia on Friday 7 December 1787. The convict woman with whom he fathered a daughter on Norfolk Island was Mary Branham.

Robert Hamilton Mathews (1841–1918), mentioned in the discussion of William Dawes, was an Australian-born surveyor, and later deputy coroner of Parramatta. Surveying for twenty years in northern New South Wales, he interviewed Aboriginal people about their language, social structure, ceremonial life and art. He recorded the story of Mirragan and Gurangatch mentioned in my final chapter, 'Showing off'. Historian Martin Thomas has recently completed the first book-length study of his life, *The Many Worlds of RH Mathews: In Search of an Australian Anthropologist* (to be published by Allen & Unwin in 2011).

Elizabeth Macarthur's well-known description of Dawes is taken from page 120 of Martin Thomas's *The Artificial Horizon: Imagining the Blue Mountains* (Melbourne: University of Melbourne Press, 2003).

Ross Gibson's essay, 'Event-Grammar: The Language Notebooks of William Dawes', was published in *Meanjin*, Volume 68, Number 2,

2009. Thank you to Ross for answering a query about this work.

Crosley's description of finding barely any trace of Dawes's observatory is recorded by Andrew James (2008) in his 'Southern Astronomical Delights' website: www.homepage.mac.com/andjames/Page03Ib.htm. Thanks to Andrew for sourcing this quote for me to the Papers of the Board of Longitude in the Royal Greenwich Observatory Archives, London (Reference: RGO 14/68), 1787–1824.

Farmer's Department Store on Market Street is now Grace Brothers; it installed the first plate-glass windows in NSW in 1854. The official name of the store that was opened in 1905 on Pitt, George and Goulburn streets was 'The Palace Emporium', though I only ever heard it referred to by Sydneysiders as 'Anthony Hordern's'. When its rival Waltons acquired it and closed it in 1970, the tree on the Hordern family estate in Camden – on which the store's crest, with its motto 'While I live I'll grow', was based – famously died. Mark Foy's 'Piazza' opened in 1908, and soon spawned new buildings to house other departments; it was acquired by Waltons in 1972, and was later leased by Grace Brothers in 1980, closing its doors in

1983. It was transformed into the Sydney Local Court, where I observed trials as an Arts-Law student. At least one of the other subsidiary buildings has been converted into apartments.

Ruth Park's description of the old woman feeding stray cats in Essex Street is taken from her *Companion Guide to Sydney*, page 54.

Harry Seidler's infamous Blues Point Tower was built in 1962, the first high-rise strata title building in the world.

On the radiation poisoning of properties in Nelson Street Hunters Hill – untreated, and undisclosed, by the NSW government when it sold the land to private parties – see Ben Cubby, 'Luxury Home is too Radioactive to Live in', *Sydney Morning Herald*, 25 June 2008. The uranium smelter that operated here had closed in 1916. (Ironically, one set of owners bought a property here in 2001 to develop into their 'dream home' from the Health Department. The radioactivity of the soil next to their bedroom was measured at 350 times higher than the acceptable level.) See, also, Ben Cubby, 'State Tried to Pass on Contamination Costs', *Sydney Morning Herald*, 2 February 2008. According to this article, a 1965 survey had found high levels of gamma-ray radiation on the site but residential construction had been allowed to go ahead nevertheless. Public concern about the site was first raised in the 1970s. Several past residents of the area, one of whom lived in the house affectionately nicknamed 'Radium', have come forward with stories of becoming ill after eating vegetables grown on the site, and deaths from cancer.

For a discussion of the 2006 warning against eating fish from Sydney Harbour, see Jonathan Harley, 'Sydney Pollution Prompts Fishing Ban' (transcript of ABC's '7.30 Report', 25 January 2006 www.abc.net.au/7.30/content/2006/s1555375.htm.

The Reverend Frank Cash's *Parables of the Harbour Bridge: Setting Forth the Preparation for, and Progressive Growth of, the Sydney Harbour Bridge, to April, 1930*, was published in 1930 (Sydney: SD Townsend). All quotes from this edition. My reference to God's earth that 'abideth forever' is from Ecclesiastes 1.4. There is also a sense in which Cash may be associating modernity with the destruction of the old, an idea embodied by Baron Haussman who, in creating the new Paris of wide boulevards to replace the medieval city, conferred on himself the title of 'demolition artist' (*artiste démolisseur*).

Emile Mercier was born in New Caledonia in

1901 and died in 1981. I still have on my shelves a treasured and battered copy of his *Sauce or Mustard?* (Sydney: Angus & Robertson, 1951). While he is most associated with *Smith's Weekly*, these cartoons are taken from his work for the *Sun*. *Gravy Pie* was published by Angus & Robertson in 1953.

Peter Carey's novel *Illywhacker* (Brisbane: University of Queensland Press) was first published in 1985.

Joseph Cindric's trolley — or one of them, for he made several over the course of his forty years on the streets — is in the Powerhouse Museum collection, and can be viewed at www.dhub.org/object/143429. Donated by the Bennelong Nursing Home, it is a poignant testament to loneliness. It was also the inspiration for a number of artworks in homage to Cindric by artist Richard Goodwin.

Kenneth Slessor's 'The Lane' was published in the *Daily Telegraph*, 26 October 1962, and reproduced in his *Bread and Wine: Selected Prose* (Sydney: Angus & Robertson, 1970).

The story about ships' anchors being heard from tunnels beneath the harbour floor is related by one of Ruth Park's sources in her *Companion Guide to Sydney*, page 363.

Yevgeny Yevtushenko's description of Adelaide as a 'cafeteria built on a graveyard' is related by Hal Porter in the third volume of his autobiography, *The Extra* (Sydney: Angus and Robertson, 1967, page 113). Porter's book also contains a stunningly bitchy description of Kenneth Slessor, living on bad terms with his second wife in their home on the Pacific Highway in Chatswood, during his last years.

Patrick White's *Voss* was published in 1957, *The Vivisector* in 1968. 'Lulworth' is now 'St Luke's' in Roslyn Gardens, Elizabeth Bay.

In his memoir *The Land I Came Through Last* (Sydney: Giramondo, 2008), poet Robert Gray offers a hilarious portrait of the theatrical self-parody theatre White and Lascaris offered fellow bus-goers in their later years.

David Marr's description of Patrick White's scruffy final resting place in Centennial Park is from his *Patrick White: A Life* (Sydney: Random House, 1991, page 644).

The story of the Luna Park fire is taken from Sam Marshall's *Luna Park: Just for Fun* (Sydney: Luna Park Reserve Trust, 1995).

Martin Sharp's film, *Street of Dreams*, has a nominal date of 1988, and occasionally turns up at film festivals – but is yet to be released. Sharp also produced iconic pop art renditions of Arthur Stace's 'Eternity', and his posters for the old Nimrod Theatre, featuring a stylised 'Mo' (entertainer Mo McCackie, aka Roy Rene) still grace many inner-city lounge rooms. For the description of the Ghost Train fire memorial, see Sean Nicholls, 'Ghost Train Memorial Tree Haunts Developers', *Sydney Morning Herald*, 14 July 2003. One of the Park's directors, Warwick Doughty, dismissed the bench, painted by Kingston, and misplaced in the $72 million development, as 'one of those cheap seats you buy in a hardware store'. It has been replaced by a small plaque; and in 2007 North Sydney Council created a separate memorial park.

Living

Information on the life of Branwhite Clarke is taken from Elena Grainger, *The Remarkable Reverend Clarke: The Life and Times of the Father of Australian Geology* (Melbourne: Oxford University Press, 1982). Clarke's description of Sydney's coves can be found on page 76, and the distress he recorded in his journal at leaving Dorsetshire ('Vesuvius in eruption') on page 58; 'sermons in stones' on page 64; his description of the large corroboree on pages

98–99; the entry 'tonight I sleep without crying' on page 100. When he left for Sydney Clarke had believed he would be appointed to the curacy of the parish of Campbelltown; but on arriving, he was reassigned to the King's School. He could only keep up this punishing schedule of teaching five and half days a week then ministering on the weekend, for a year; afterward he resigned from the headmastership and worked solely as a minister. He became rector of Campbelltown in 1844, and then moved to St Thomas's in North Sydney in 1846, where he remained until his retirement in 1871.

Sumner Locke Elliott's indictment of Arncliffe's 'commonness' appears in his novel *Fairyland* (Sydney: Picador, 1991), on pages 33–34.

Martin Thomas discusses the mysteries surrounding his own house in Pennant Hills, 'staring blankly at its neighbours', in *The Artificial Horizon*, page 36.

The stories about the history of Roseville Chase – of colonial surgeon John White's meeting with an old Aboriginal man, Bate's farm, and Stefan and Genowefa Pietroszys – come from Gavin Souter's lovely history of Middle Harbour, *Times and Tides: A Middle Harbour Memoir* (Sydney: Simon

& Schuster, 2004). The first description of Bate's farm is from page 67; the text of the real estate advertisement from page 74. I am also indebted to Professor Paul Ashton, at UTS, for sharing with me his research on Echo Point.

Gerard Manley Hopkins, 'Pied Beauty', can be found in Gerard Manley Hopkins, *Poems and Prose*, selected by WH Gardner (London: Penguin, 1963, pages 30–31).

Lawrence Weschler's essay 'The Light of LA' can be found in his collection of essays, *Vermeer in Bosnia* (New York: Pantheon Books, 2004, pages 300–15).

The 1985 film adaptation of Peter Carey's novel, *Bliss*, was directed by Ray Lawrence and produced by the NSW Film Corporation.

Lantana, also directed by Ray Lawrence, was produced by the Australian Film Finance Corporation, and was released in 2001.

For a fascinating insight into the continuing traditions of the Cammeraigal (Gai-mariagal) in northern Sydney – including the descriptions of sites around the Narrabeen Lakes area mentioned in this chapter – see Dennis Foley, *Repossession of Our Spirit: Traditional Owners of Northern Sydney* (Canberra: Aboriginal History, 2001 – Aboriginal History

Monograph Number 7). The Cammeraigal country extended from the boundaries of the Lane Cove River system in the west, across the ridge between Terrey Hills and Duffys Forest, to Mona Vale in the north; this coastal territory extends south all the way down to Middle Cove, North Sydney and back round to Chatswood. Quite astonishingly, to a white reader, Foley describes how knowledge was being passed on to him by elders in the bush, and how some of his people still occupied traditional camps, into the 1960s.

Peter Butt puts forward the theory of poisoning by toxic river gases in his documentary, *Who Killed Dr Bogle and Mrs Chandler?* It was produced by Film Australia and Blackwattle films, and aired on the ABC on 7 September 2006.

The description of the drive from St Ives to Sydney's northern beaches in Malcolm Knox's novel *Summerland* (Sydney: Random House, 2000) can be found on pages 16–17.

The German-Jewish philosopher and sociologist Walter Benjamin described the sensation of suddenly finding oneself in a new area of Paris as crossing a low step in his *Arcades Project* (Cambridge, Massachusetts: Belknap Press, 1999, translated by Howard Eiland and Kevin McLaughlin).

'Nowhere, unless perhaps in dreams', writes Benjamin, 'can the phenomenon of the boundary be experienced in a more originary way than in cities ... As threshold, the boundary stretches across streets; a new precinct begins like a step in the void – as though one had unexpectedly cleared a low step on a flight of stairs' (page 88).

The twelve-part documentary television series 'Sylvania Waters', which offered a fly-on-the-wall peek into the life of couple Noeline Baker and Laurie Donaher, premiered on ABC TV in 1992. Produced by Paul Watson and Pamela Wilson, it was a co-production with the BBC.

Both the Nepean and Gross rivers are tributaries of the Hawkesbury River. All quotes are taken from the online version of Watkin Tench's *Complete Account of the Settlement at Port Jackson, in New South Wales*. However, to make it clear that this is the same Colebe I mention in my opening chapter, I have retained the spelling of Colebe's name from the *Australian Dictionary of Biography*; Boladaree and Gomberee's names are as Tench rendered them.

In regard to the pronunciation of the cicada 'Yellow Monday' as 'Yellah Mundee', I have polled friends from interstate, and none recalls using this second pronunciation, whereas friends from my own city do; this strengthens my sense that the name has taken on associations peculiar to the Sydney area.

Frances Bodkin's book about Sydney's weather systems, illustrated by Lorraine Roberston, is *D'harawal Seasons and Climate Cycles* (Sydney: F Bodkin and L Robertson, 2008). Bodkin was able to interview 106 Dharawal descendants on condition that she identified interviewees by numbers only, and her notes were handwritten, not tape recorded. The interview with Bodkin from which I have quoted is a feature from 'The Lab', a site produced by the ABC's Science division. It was published on 13 August 2003, www.abc.net.au/science/features/indigenous/.

The material about Anita Cobby is taken from Julia Shepherd's *Someone Else's Daughter: The Life and Death of Anita Cobby* (Sydney: Ironbark Press, 1991).

Patrick White described the southerly blowing into 'Dogwoods' 'with a roar like the sea' in a letter to Peggy Garland, quoted on page 265 of David Marr's *Patrick White: A Life*. Marr's description of Castle Hill's 'no-hopers and mad women' is on page 268. White described himself as feeling like and alien and 'foreigner' in *Patrick White Speaks*, quoted on page 383 of Marr. It may seem hard to believe in multicultural Sydney that being of Greek extraction could have been so remarkable, but, as White pointed out in a 1964 letter to Marshall Best (Marr, 269), 'Australians are always amazed when they meet Manoly, simply because the only Greeks they have ever come across are fishmongers and milk-bar proprietors'. Patrick White's description of an Australia in which 'the mind is the least of possessions' is from his 1958 essay 'Prodigal Son', quoted by Marr on page 277.

The description of Amy and Stan walking in the garden after the children had been fed is from Patrick White, *The Tree of Man* (Harmondsworth: Penguin, 1973, page 147); the novel was originally published by Eyre and Spottiswoode in 1956, and is dedicated 'To Manoly'. The description of Stan Parker, 'full of wonder', in the storm appears on page 151. *Riders in the Chariot* was first published in 1961 by the Viking Press. Quote about Miss Hare, from this edition, pages 34–35.

White's remarks about the 'surface' nature of life in Sydney on his return (written to his cousin Peggy Garland) are taken from David Malouf's 'Patrick White Appraised', *Sydney Morning Herald*, 27 January 2007. Thanks to Barbara Mobbs for permission to use all Patrick White quotes.

Sweating

The classification of Sydney sandstone by Pyrmont's quarrymen into the categories 'hellhole' (hard), 'purgatory' and 'paradise' (easy to cut, and a beautiful gold colour once out of the ground), is referred to by interviewee Ron Powell in 'Sydney Sandstone', ABC TV's 'Dimensions in Time' program for 10 December 2003. It can be found on the ABC's 'Sydney Sidetracks' site, a wonderful online source of clips from ABC TV and radio programs: www.abc.net.au/innovation/sidetracks/downloads.htm.

Ken Unsworth's *Stones Against the Sky* was installed in front of the 'Elan' apartments on Darlinghurst Road, Kings Cross in 1998. The artist has apparently virtually disowned the sculpture, after the developers failed to execute his intentions to surround the poles by living gum trees; and they used fibreglass, rather than stone, to make the 'stones'.

The ecstatic description of the harbour around Watsons Bay in Christina Stead's *For Love Alone* (Sydney: Angus and Robertson, 1966) appears on page 61.

Rayner Hoff's ANZAC War Memorial was completed in 1934. (Hoff had taught Guy Lynch, the sculptor of *Satyr*.) But returned servicemen never embraced this memorial; instead Sir Bertram Mackennal's more traditional Cenotaph in Martin Place, dedicated in 1927, has remained the popular site of commemorative events.

Ruth Park describes her life with D'Arcy Niland in Surry Hills in *Fishing in the Styx*. It seems that the readers incensed by *The Harp in the South* were objecting not so much to its frankness about the harshness of slum life, or accidental pregnancy and abortion, but the fact that Park had depicted slum residents as normal, rather than crooks and thugs. After its 1946 serialisation, the novel was published by Angus & Robertson in 1948.

Mandy Sayer on Plunkett St Public, Woolloomooloo: 'Urban Goddess', *Wentworth Courier*, 14 November 2007, page 11.

Material on gay Sydney, including the Archibald Fountain beat, and early colonial law, is taken from Robert French's *Camping by a Billabong* (Sydney: Blackwattle Press, 1993). Lord Beauchamp's enthusiastic quote appears on page 45.

Vince Kelly was the author of *Rugged Angel: The Amazing Career of Policewoman Lillian Armfield* (Sydney: Angus and Robertson, 1961).

The account of the 1978 Mardi Gras Riot is taken from Liz Ross, 'It was a Riot! 30 Years Since

Australia's First Mardi Gras', *Socialist Alternative*. 11 February 2008. The eyewitness who recounts shouting 'Up the Lezzos' is unnamed.

'Axis of Sequins', (no author), appeared in the *Sydney Morning Herald* on 1 March 2003.

Robert Hughes refers to our convict history as 'vivid, trashy Grand Guignol' on page xiii of his *The Fatal Shore: A History of the Transportation of Convicts to Australia, 1787–1868* (London: Collins Harvill, 1987).

The material on Sydney's 'preindustrial' eighteenth-century history and The Rocks is taken from Grace Karskens, *The Rocks: Life in Early Sydney* (Melbourne: Melbourne University Publishing, 1997).

Fred Nile's remark, 'If Jesus wept…' is quoted by David Marr in 'The Power of One', *Sydney Morning Herald*, 5 January 2008.

Jessica Anderson's *Tirra Lirra by the River* was published in 1978. Quotes are from the 1997 Picador edition. 'If I had to live here I would die' page 51; 'a woman's figure has to be ruined…' pages 63–64.

Alan Saffron's account of his father's Kings Cross activities is *Gentle Satan: My Father, Abe Saffron* (Melbourne: Penguin, 2008).

The 1976 ABC report on Juanita Nielsen's disappearance, including the interview with the real estate agent – and other video resources on the case (including the radio interview with residents) – can be found on the ABC's 'Sydney Sidetracks' site. Interviews with residents referred to are from the excellent 1977 Double J radio program, 'The Battle for Victoria Street', and the interview with the real estate agent from ABC TV's 'This Day Tonight', 1976.

Peter Rees's *Killing Juanita: A True Story of Murder and Corruption in King's Cross* was published by Allen & Unwin in 2004.

Sydney photographer and performer William Yang told the story of Peter Tully's 'Tragic Tourist' tour in his theatrical/documentary presentation, *My Generation*, which I attended at Carriageworks in 2010. Yang's books of photographs include *Sadness* (Sydney: Allen & Unwin, 1996) and *Patrick White: The Late Years* (Sydney: Pan Macmillan, 1995). Thanks to William for generously emailing me this section of his script and allowing me to quote from it.

Showing off

Customs House was built in 1896, replacing an earlier sandstone building. The infamous 'Dictation Test' was the cornerstone of the White Australia Policy: customs officers around the country had the power from 1901 to exclude all non-Europeans, and, in the face of international criticism, used the test as a means of obfuscating the fact that exclusions were made on the base of race. The practice continued into the 1960s. Although the building remained the home of the Customs service until 1990, most of its operations had moved to Darling Harbour mid-century, although officers were kept busy in the 1960s at the Overseas Terminal (which is now the location of many bars and restaurants) on the west side of the Quay, processing new immigrants. The old Maritime Services building behind it is now the Museum of Contemporary Art (MCA).

There is beautiful ABC news footage from 1960 of the Sicilian fishermen of Woolloomooloo drying their nets in Palmer Street on its 'Sydney Sidetracks' website. See 'Fishing in the 'Loo'.

Joseph Conrad's *Heart of Darkness* (New York: Modern Library, 1999) first appeared as a three-part series in *Blackwood's Magazine* in 1899, before being published in book form in 1902.

The administrator's remark that 'everyone' could feel at home in Edelsten's opulent centres is from Rosalind Reines's article, 'Medicare with a Sugar Coating' (*Sydney Morning Herald*, 4 March 1985). Thanks to Susan Wyndham at the *Sydney Morning Herald* for digging clippings on Edelsten's Medical Centres out of the archive for me.

Material on the Sydney International Exhibition of 1879 is drawn from Peter Proudfoot, Roslyn Maguire and Robert Freestone (eds), *Colonial City, Global City: Sydney's International Exhibition 1879* (Sydney: Crossing Press, 2000). Ethel Pockley's 22 September 1882 eyewitness description of the fire appears on page 218. JC Hoyte's 1882 watercolour *The Burning of the Garden Palace* is in the Mitchell Library, State Library of NSW.

Terry Durack's description of the Manly Pavilion is from 'Italian With an Aussie Accent', *Sydney Morning Herald*, 'Good Living' supplement, 6 April 2010, page 5. Ironically, Sydney's affair with the Tuscan has been blamed for contributing to our water crisis. According to a 2003 report in the same paper (Stephanie Peatling, 'Paving the Way to a Flood of Run-off', 5 August 2003), Sydney's paved parterre gardens, extensive terraces and sweeping driveways, have been wasting millions of litres of usable water a year, as water that was once soaked up by gardens rushes off hard surfaces and into stormwater run-off − picking up litter, bacteria, oils and metals on its way to the harbour.

Dennis Foley mentions the Gidgingal on page 10 of *Repossession of Our Spirit: Traditional Owners of Northern Sydney* although, he writes, '[t]heir dreaming is under water and we rarely speak openly of them'.

The Maori oarsmen who rowed the harbour pilots from their post at Watsons Bay are mentioned on page 78 of Ian Hoskins's *Sydney Harbour: A History* (Sydney: University of New South Wales Press, 2009).

Material on the life of Mei Quong Tart is taken from Robert Travers's *Australian Mandarin: The Life and Times of Quong Tart* (Sydney: Rosenberg Publishing, 2004). Although 'Mei' was his family name, the tea merchant was always known in Sydney as 'Quong Tart', or simply 'Quong'. The two policemen who caught Quong Tart's attacker would later go on to international fame for their immaculate police work in tracking down and apprehending the 'Blue Mountains murderer'.

Ivor Indyk discusses Kenneth Slessor's

relationship to his Jewish-German family history in his 'Kenneth Slessor's "Five Bells"' in the *Australian Literary Compendium*: www.australianliterarycompendium.com/fivebellsessay.html. Slessor's father had been born Robert Schloesser, in England, and changed the family's name during the Great War. Slessor's mother's family were from the Hebrides.

Kenneth Slessor makes his reference to the old 'bunch-of-bananas' city in his 'Portrait of Sydney', page 71.

The source for the quote from Mayor Frank Sartor about the copyrighting of Stace's 'Eternity' is a Sydney City Council emailed media release dated 12 January 2001, reproduced at: www.pastornet.net.au/stace/News.htm.

Hans Bandler, the chief design engineer of Warragamba Dam, was a Viennese Jew, and the survivor of two notorious concentration camps. His monograph is *Warragamba and Burragorang: A History of Two Submerged, Confluent Valleys* (The Oaks, NSW: The Oaks Historical Society, 1995).

The use by flying foxes of roads like Anzac Parade, in order to navigate to their feeding grounds, is mentioned by Anna Funder in her short essay 'Bad Hotel', *The Monthly*, April 2010.

Acknowledgments

Thanks to Phillipa McGuinness for approaching me to write this book; to my editors Judith Lukin-Amundsen and Fiona Sim; and Naomi Parry and Martin Thomas, Simeon Barlow, Ronn Morris and Brenda Walker for generously reading this work in manuscript (the errors are my own). Thanks, too, to my other dear friends, for kindnesses over the last few years; also to colleagues, especially John Dale, at the University of Technology, Sydney. Love always, and deep gratitude, to Richard Harling; and to my mother, who taught me to see this city.

WINDSOR

CASTLE HILL

Shirley Road

Pacific Highway

Warringah Freeway

Kurraba Rd

Milson Ro

L O W E R   N O

McMAHONS POINT

Luna Park Sydney

Sydney Harbour Bridge

BALMAIN

Dawes Point

Sydney Opera House

Darling St

BARANGAROO

Cahill Expressway

Royal Botanic Gardens

PENRITH

PYRMONT

C I T Y

P
P

BLUE MOUNTAINS

WOOLLOOMOOLOO

FLEMINGTON

Western Distributor

York St

KINGS CROSS

ELI
BAY

ROOKWOOD CEMETERY

GLEBE

Elizabeth Street

DARLINGH

Parramatta Road

Anzac Parade

CHIPPENDALE

I N N E R
W E S T

Gibbons St

THE SUTHERLAND